Leading and Managing

A Differentiated Classroom

2nd Edition

ASCD MEMBER BOOK

Many ASCD members received this book as a
member benefit upon its initial release.

Learn more at: **www.ascd.org/memberbooks**

Carol Ann Tomlinson
Marcia B. Imbeau

Leading and Managing
A Differentiated Classroom
2nd Edition

Arlington, Virginia USA

2800 Shirlington Road, Suite 1001 • Arlington, VA 22206 USA
Phone: 800-933-2723 or 703-578-9600 • Fax: 703-575-5400
Website: www.ascd.org • Email: member@ascd.org
Author guidelines: www.ascd.org/write

Penny Reinart, *Deputy Executive Director*; Genny Ostertag, *Managing Director, Book Acquisitions & Editing*; Mary Beth Nielsen, *Interim Director, Book Editing*; Katie Martin, *Editor*; Thomas Lytle, *Creative Director*; Donald Ely, *Art Director*; Georgia Park, *Senior Graphic Designer*; Valerie Younkin, *Senior Production Designer*; Kelly Marshall, *Production Manager*; Shajuan Martin, *E-Publishing Specialist*; Christopher Logan, *Senior Production Specialist*

Figure 2.1 on page 51 is used with permission from *Differentiation and the Brain: How Neuroscience Supports the Learner-Friendly Classroom* by David A. Sousa and Carol Ann Tomlinson. Solution Tree Press, 555 North Morton Street, Bloomington, IN 47404, 800.733.6786. All rights reserved. Solution Tree is a leading provider of educational strategies and tools that improve staff and student performance. Visit solution-tree.com for more information.

All web links in this book are correct as of the publication date below but may have become inactive or otherwise modified since that time. If you notice a deactivated or changed link, please email books@ascd.org with the words "Link Update" in the subject line. In your message, please specify the web link, the book title, and the page number on which the link appears.

PAPERBACK ISBN: 978-1-4166-3177-4   ASCD product# 122012

PDF EBOOK ISBN: 978-1-4166-3178-1; see Books in Print for other formats.

Quantity discounts are available: email programteam@ascd.org or call 800-933-2723, ext. 5773, or 703-575-5773. For desk copies, go to www.ascd.org/deskcopy.

ASCD Member Book No. FY23-3 (Dec. 2022 P). ASCD Member Books mail to Premium (P), Select (S), and Institutional Plus (I+) members on this schedule: Jan, PSI+; Feb, P; Apr, PSI+; May, P; Jul, PSI+; Aug, P; Sep, PSI+; Nov, PSI+; Dec, P. For current details on membership, see www.ascd.org/membership.

Library of Congress Cataloging-in-Publication Data
Names: Tomlinson, Carol A., author. | Imbeau, Marcia B., author.
Title: Leading and managing a differentiated classroom / Carol Ann Tomlinson, Marcia B. Imbeau.
Description: 2nd edition. | Arlington, Virginia : ASCD, 2023. | Includes bibliographical references and index.
Identifiers: LCCN 2022047464 (print) | LCCN 2022047465 (ebook) | ISBN 9781416631774 (paperback) | ISBN 9781416631781 (pdf)
Subjects: LCSH: Individualized instruction—United States. | Inclusive education—United States. | Classroom management—United States.
Classification: LCC LB1031 .T67 2023 (print) | LCC LB1031 (ebook) | DDC   371.39/4—dc23/eng/20221102
LC record available at https://lccn.loc.gov/2022047464
LC ebook record available at https://lccn.loc.gov/2022047465

32 31 30 29 28 27 26 25 24 23   1 2 3 4 5 6 7 8 9 10 11 12

For the teachers who didn't give up on us,
whose aspirations helped us find something better
in ourselves than we had seen before,
and who then, through experience and by example,
taught us the enlivening power of learning.
And to the people whose steady love compels
us to ask each time we enter a classroom,
*"Which person in this place is **not** in need*
of the same sense of possibility these teachers have given us?"

Leading and Managing a Differentiated Classroom

2nd Edition

Preface

Far away there in the sunshine are my highest aspirations. I may not reach them, but I can look up and see their beauty, believe in them, and try to follow where they lead.

—Louisa May Alcott

I couldn't tell you much in detail about my sixth year of teaching, or my tenth, or any other specific year in the 21 years I spent in high school, preschool, and middle school classrooms except for my first and fourth years. There are memories from each of the years I taught in public school that will always reside in me, of course, but no other particular years exist in my mind with the sharp detail of those two. It was in those two years that I established my compass as a teacher.

As a teenager, I vowed I'd never be a teacher. My mother was a teacher (and immensely proud of her work), which was fine with me—until she and I ended up in the same school during my 6th grade year. It was a hard year for me. Not only was I entering adolescence with an impressive case of self-consciousness, but I was also attending a new school in a new town. On principle, I didn't *want* to like anything. My teacher that year was one of the best I ever had. Nonetheless, it was clear to me that my mother came home with knowledge of things I had said or done during the school day. I felt spied on, and that nourished my self-consciousness. With the lack of logic that is adolescence, I concluded that I did not want to be one of those "spy people" who watched kids and told on them. (Forget that my teacher was supportive and kind and tried to make my life better; in my adolescent mind, she was a spy … and I was the one spied upon.)

So, I declared I would do anything but teach when I grew up. Over the next 10 years, I persisted with that declaration at appropriate points—including when my mother suggested I take education courses in college, "just in case." With some disdain, I reminded my mother that I was a young adult who had earned the right to make her own decisions. In turn, my mother explained, with remarkable calmness, that *she* was the one paying my college tuition bill. She would support any major I chose so long as I took the education courses required for certification.

I took the education courses. As expected, I found them pointless and renewed my vow that I would never, ever, under any circumstances be a teacher.

A Career Begins

I got my first job as a teacher in my second year out of college. I was working as an advertising manager for a university press, and despite my natural introversion, I just couldn't warm up to a job that called on me to sit alone in a small room, day after day, working with esoteric copy for esoteric books. Then, at lunch one day in October, I saw a newspaper ad for a teaching job. Magically, it sounded like salvation. I took the afternoon off, went for the interview, and was hired on a one-year contract to be a high school English and history teacher.

On Monday, I arrived at my new K–12 school, which was about an hour and 15 minutes from my house. It was in an area that gave sharp definition to the word *rural*. The little town had a name, a post office, a flue shop (it sold tobacco-curing supplies), and an autobody shop. The post office closed shortly after I arrived because it had too little business. The flue shop fared well enough because of the local tobacco growers. The body shop thrived because of its location: near a railroad track where the road dipped about 12 inches with no warning.

The principal of the school where I was about to begin what I assumed would be a one-year career seldom came to school during the early part of the day. He was shy and, I think, quite afraid of the older students. So it was the assistant principal who took me to my new classroom on Day 1 and announced to the very small, elderly teacher in the classroom that he was fired. Understandably angry, the teacher told me that, since he was no longer employed, I should jump right in and see what *I* could do with the class. Despite befuddled terror and my own massive shyness, I found enough voice to say to him that I'd been promised a day to observe and get textbooks before I started teaching, and so I believed it would be better if I just sat in the back of the room.

And that's what I did. For the rest of the day, I watched as high school girls giggled and chatted and high school boys crawled in and out of the first-floor window and tried (unsuccessfully) to set a large freestanding bulletin board on fire. Two thoughts kept playing on a loop in my mind: "What am I going to do with this chaos tomorrow?" and "I don't think I need a job this badly."

Recall that, as a college student, I found my education classes to be without merit. Whether that was the result of the classes themselves or of my attitude about taking them, the reality of my new situation was that I had no idea how to teach. Yet this seemed less important than the realization that I had not the first clue about how to "manage" the high school students who were clearly in need of "being managed."

In my overwrought condition, I completed my very first lesson plan at 3:42 a.m. on Tuesday morning. It was a truly stupid plan that seemed completely acceptable at the time: I would have the students complete a crossword puzzle with me. The intent of the plan was twofold. First, it would buy me a day to figure out what these students knew and didn't know about American literature and world history—the two subjects I had been hired to teach. Second, it would let me establish myself as someone who gave clear and effective directions to students so we would have order in the classroom—in other words, I'd be able to keep the kids in their seats.

This crossword puzzle had very little to do with either literature or history. Its main qualification for my first lesson plan was that it was the only crossword puzzle I could find in the middle of the night. It provided no window at all into my students' knowledge of our content, and my thought that they would follow directions simply because I gave them was beyond naïve.

By all rights, my first day as a teacher should have been a cosmic disaster. Instead, it taught me the first of many lessons I learned that year that have continued to serve me well ever since.

Classroom Management 101, Lesson 1

It turned out that my students were from a universe largely unrelated to the one I knew. Most of them had never left the insular area where they had been born. None of them had college-educated parents, and few of them had any aspirations for a career—or even a job. With little meaningful interaction with the wider world, old suspicions and animosities permeated their community. "Outsiders" didn't show up there very often. And yet these students were happy, thoughtful, full of a wisdom the likes of which I had never encountered, and wide open to new possibilities, despite the fact that they were pretty sure I was from an alien planet.

On my first Tuesday as a teacher, I got my students' attention when I asked them to take assigned seats as they entered the room. This caught them off guard; they were unaccustomed to having assigned seats, and for a moment, the surprise made them uncharacteristically quiet. Quiet was promising! Then I passed out copies of the crossword puzzle, explaining to students that they would work in pairs on specified portions of the puzzle, and after a while, we would reassemble as a whole class to check the portion of the work they had completed. My plan was to solve the entire puzzle in stages: work in pairs, come together, check work, then go back to the pairs to solve another portion. It was less a lesson plan than choreography of a teacher giving directions and students following them.

The big, unanticipated problem was that not a single one of my 10th grade students had ever seen a crossword puzzle, let alone solved one. They turned the purple ditto sheets over and over as if they were seeking some sort of physical orientation to the task. Realization dawning, I adjusted my plans accordingly: I'd just give directions to the class as a whole, and we'd solve the entire puzzle together. After all, the answers to the crossword puzzle were secondary, weren't they? What mattered was that I gave good directions and that the students followed them. What mattered was that I maintained order.

I hit another, more serious roadblock when I read the first clue aloud. It said, "Our country, abbr." The puzzle had three blank boxes for the answer. In the moment that followed, my students' faces and a few verbal hints revealed the following: (1) no one knew what the clues had to do with the boxes, (2) there might have been some confusion about the meaning of "across" versus "down," (3) no one knew what an abbreviation was (yielding a serious problem with the abbreviation of *abbreviation*), and, most significantly, (4) not a single student seemed to know the name of our country. After a painful sequence of hint-fueled guesses had finally led us to "the United States of America," we encountered a fifth problem—a country with a four-part name but only three boxes to enter its abbreviation. All five of my classes that day ended with me announcing, as the bell rang, that our country was called the United States of America and the abbreviation for that name was USA. It took an entire class period, but we were finally ready to enter an answer for 1-Across. But do you know what? The students stayed in their seats.

At the end of the day, I was exhausted, delighted with the extreme orderliness of my classes, and devoid of ideas about what I should do on Wednesday. Although I was also too tired and too new to understand what I had just learned, my first principle of classroom management eventually became clear: *When students are engaged, they have no motivation to misbehave.* My students were models of deportment on that day—not because I stood in front of them and gave directions, of course, but because I had happened onto a task (albeit a vacuous one) that intrigued them.

Classroom Management 101, Lesson 2

My education as a teacher continued throughout the year, with a second pivotal lesson about classroom management coming about two weeks later. In the interim, my students and I had good moments and bad. Although I was trying hard, I truly didn't know what I was doing. I couldn't steer a steady course because I didn't yet know why some things worked and others didn't.

It was to my advantage that I was a novelty for the students—a very tall teacher from the outside world who continued to do the unexpected in a school where nearly all the faculty were "lifers" in the community. I continued to use seating charts, and I was still big on making sure I gave clear directions for my unorthodox assignments. That's what I was attempting to do during first period on a Monday when, about 10 minutes after the tardy bell, a formidable-looking girl entered the classroom by slamming the door against the wall. She stood in the threshold with her hands on her hips and an "I dare you to mess with me" look on her face.

The rest of the class looked wide-eyed at the student in the doorway, their expressions telling me both that they knew who this was and that they were not about to mess with her. A switch flipped in my head, and I recalled that there was a student in this class who'd been absent since I arrived. I smiled at the girl in the doorway and greeted her. "I bet you're Estralita," I said. "I'm Carol Tomlinson, and I'm the new teacher for this class. Everyone has an assigned seat now, and yours is right up here." I pointed to a vacant seat in the front row. She stared for another second or two, emitted a sound that can only be described as a snort, and headed for the back of the room.

What happened next could have gone in a very different direction. Again, I smiled broadly at Estralita and said mildly, "We've missed you, Estralita. I'm glad you're back. Now get your sorry self in your assigned seat up here so you can work with us." Then I immediately launched back into the assignment directions. The class inhaled collectively. Estralita's eyes flashed. She looked around, puzzled, I think, by the sight of all of her classmates sitting there *not* misbehaving. Estralita stopped, pivoted, and then stalked to the front of the room. She threw her books on the floor and sat in desk like an angry bull for the rest of the class. I smiled at her again as the period ended and told her I was looking forward to getting to know her. Her only reply was another one of those snorts.

The next day was a rerun of this scenario. Estralita bashed in about 10 minutes into class, and I smiled at her and said, "I'm so glad you came today; I was afraid you were absent." Again, the class froze. Again, Estralita stared and headed with a harrumph toward the back of the class. Once again, I said, "Estralita, get your sorry self in your assigned seat" and continued without pause with what I had been saying. And once again, she surveyed the territory, noticed that the class was with me, stalked to the front of the room, and deposited herself in the designated seat.

We continued this perilous ballet for four days. By Friday, all the moves were predictable. As Estralita propelled herself to the rear of the room, I began my now well-rehearsed response, "Estralita . . . ."

"I know," she said, interrupting me. "I gotta get my sorry self in my assigned seat."

And she did. At the time, I didn't realize that something important had happened; I just plowed ahead. In that moment, though, Estralita decided to join us. She made the choice to be a member of the class rather than a combatant.

Again, I didn't know for several months the importance of Estralita's decision in my survival as a teacher, and it was good that I didn't. It would have undone my fragile sense of efficacy. Much later in the year, I learned that Estralita had missed my first week in the classroom due to suspension. In fact, she had argued with the teacher I replaced and literally knocked him unconscious to the floor. I had been hired not because I had great credentials in English (and clearly not because I knew history) but because I was physically large enough to confront Estralita.

In the end, however, it was not my size that won the day with Estralita. It was her sense that I was somehow accepting of her—that I felt she belonged in the class and that there was a place for her there. In time, I came to understand my second lesson of classroom management: *If students understand that their teacher sees them as worthwhile people with significant potential, it opens doors to learning.*

My "get your sorry self in your assigned seat" comment could be seen as challenging or sarcastic. It was, however, delivered with a sincere smile and a sense of endearment. She saw in my face and heard in my tone that something had changed in this classroom. For the first time she could remember, someone was greeting her with positive expectations. It took weeks, if not months, for Estralita to truly begin trusting me, but from our first encounter, she felt invited. That was enough to buy us both some time—and to teach me once again that my penchant for directions was not enough to make me an effective "classroom manager."

Classroom Management 101, Lesson 3

I learned many more lessons about life and "managing" a classroom during that first year as a teacher. I learned how to pace lessons, how to organize materials, how to start and stop class with purpose, and how to shift gears if something wasn't going well, to name just a few. When the year ended and I moved to another state, it was hard to leave Estralita and her peers. I still think about them nearly four decades later.

My second year as a teacher was spent as the director of and teacher in a preschool with a very international population in a metropolitan area. Once again, I had no idea what I was doing. Once again, I learned important lessons through instinct, error, and luck. Once again, my students taught me more than I was prepared to teach them.

It was in my third setting, this time in a district where I would go on to teach for 20 years, that my third career-shaping lesson about "managing" a classroom presented itself. As had been the case with my first two schools, the student population pushed on the perimeter of my experiences. In this school, we had a bimodal population. By that, I mean that nearly 50 percent of the students in my 7th grade language arts classes read four or more years *below* grade level, and nearly 50 percent of them read four or more years *above* grade level. In other words, there were almost no students "in the middle."

At this point in my development, I finally believed I was a teacher. The students had not devoured me in terms of "classroom management" during my initial years, and now I even had a clear sense of my curriculum, thanks to a thick teacher's guide I developed with some of my colleagues during the summer after my first year in the school. Gone were the days of staying up late on Monday to figure out what to teach on Tuesday and then staying up late on Tuesday to figure out what to teach on Wednesday. With my guide, I not only knew on Monday what I should teach on Tuesday, but I knew in September what I would be teaching in May. Confident that I was in control of the students and curriculum, I was jazzed about beginning of my fourth year in the classroom.

My world shifted rapidly when I met Golden, a 15-year-old who had just been placed in my second period 7th grade class. Two weeks into the school year. Golden approached me during a class change and whispered something I could not hear. The hall resonated with student talk. He was short and I was tall. He spoke with his hand over his mouth. After three tries, I said to him, "I'm so sorry, but it's really noisy and I just can't hear what you're saying. Let's try this once more. I'll bend down so I'm closer to you and I can hear better. You keep your hand down this time. I want to hear what you're trying to tell me."

What Golden was saying to me was "I can't read," and he was telling me the truth. He was three years too old for 7th grade, and he did not know the whole alphabet. For my part, I didn't know how to teach reading, but I did know that his "confession" was an act of courage and trust, and there was no way I could let him down.

In that flash of time in the hallway, a rush of questions filled my mind—and they have driven my work ever since. How do I teach reading when I've never been trained for that? How do I make this boy a respected member of the class when he can neither read nor write? Do I seat him near someone who is really smart and let that student help him? Do I try to hide the fact that he is so far behind? What materials will I use with him? How can I find time to work with him on the things he needs? How in the world will I handle report cards in a way that is not demoralizing? Perhaps my most frightening realization was that the curriculum notebook I was sure would pave the way to my success as a teacher was suddenly an encumbrance—at least in my work with Golden.

For months, I obsessed about Golden as I tried to answer these questions (and others) that wouldn't leave me alone. We made some progress, and I began to figure out a rhythm for working with him while also teaching the 35 other students in the room. Golden's needs were very different than what the curriculum anticipated, so I began to create a different curriculum for him that was embedded within the wider curriculum I had to teach everyone.

Then I thought about Jonathan. He had been in class all year. He was a good kid, he was smart and funny, and he made good grades. It was not until the early spring, though, that I really saw Jonathan for the first time. I was teaching a lesson on symbols in literature—a tricky topic for 7th graders who are often still a bit concrete in their thinking. I was proud of my concept attainment lesson on the topic. It was well planned, and the kids couldn't have responded better. After an examination of objects and photos of objects, I felt comfortable that the students were ready to name the concept we were pursuing—in this case, symbols. They offered their labels with only modest hesitation. Most students thought the objects I had shared with them in an attempt to evoke the idea of symbols should be called "signs." One suggested "trademarks." After a long silence, one final student proposed that we call them "logos."

When it was clear that no one else had any options to offer and silence overtook the class, many students literally looked across the room to Jonathan. In compliance with their silent signal to please save the teacher from all this awkwardness, he raised his hand, sighed, and said with audible weariness, "They're symbols." The other students were satisfied that this was the right answer, because it was *Jonathan's* answer.

We then tried to define the things we'd been happily investigating. The task was too ambiguous—too risky—for most students. Back then, I didn't know about Think-Pair-Share or reflective journals or even wait time, and so the silence wrapped around us again. Once more, the other students looked to Jonathan, and once again, he raised his hand. "What do *you* think a symbol is?" I asked him gratefully. Once again he sighed and offered without pause a definition he seemingly carried in his head—had carried in his head for goodness knows how many years. "A symbol," Jonathan said, "is an abstract representation of a concrete entity."

In that moment, I understood my third principle of classroom management: *The classroom can't work for anybody until it works for everybody!*

The problem wasn't that Golden had one set of needs and everyone else had another. The problem was that I had a room full of students with widely differing needs. I couldn't make the classroom work for Golden as well as it needed to because I was trying to "fit him in" around the edges of the "real" agenda. At that point, I saw clearly that my magical curriculum guide failed Jonathan as surely as it failed Golden. I somehow had to learn to plan a classroom where flexibility provided opportunity for everyone. In other words, I understood at that moment that an effective teacher is not someone who just teaches content. An effective teacher is someone who teaches content to distinct human beings, and the classroom has to work in such a way that each individual in it has a legitimate opportunity to grow as much as possible from their starting point.

I realized, then, that classroom management is the process of figuring out how to set up and orchestrate a classroom in which students sometimes work as a whole group, as small groups, and as individuals. The goal would be to have everyone work not only on things they all need to do in common but also on things that were of particular importance for their own individual growth.

This insight indicated considerable growth in me as a teacher. I had progressed from defining "classroom management" as (1) keeping kids in their seats to (2) giving good directions to (3) being rooted in engaging curriculum to (4) stemming from genuine respect for each student, and, finally, to (5) making room for individual and group needs. Each new realization built upon and broadened my understanding of what it meant to be a teacher. Each year in the classroom, each new class, and each student in those classes were catalysts for my continuing growth in understanding and practice.

In time, I came to be a little uncomfortable with the term "classroom management." I don't like being *managed* myself, and I realized that I respond much better to being *led*. Ultimately, I understood that a part of my role was leading students and managing the details and mechanics of the classroom. Therefore, I began to think about the distinction between being a leader in and a manager of the classroom. Still later, I came to understand the interdependence of learning environment, curriculum, assessment, and instruction. I understood more clearly the ways in which classroom leadership and management were part of one system and how they could enable me to use all of the classroom elements to reach each of my students.

Throughout my career, I learned to think about time, space, materials, groups, and strategies in ways that balanced content requirements and the needs of young learners. I happened upon and invented ways to make the classroom more efficient for me and more effective for my students. Likewise, I happened upon and invented ideas that appropriately met a quick demise. This book reflects much of that learning, both things worth considering and things to avoid.

Leading and Managing a Differentiated Classroom is presented in two parts. The first part focuses on what it means for a teacher to effectively *lead* students in a differentiated classroom. The second part focuses on the mechanics of *managing* a differentiated classroom. In practice, of course, teachers must think about both elements at once. It's likely, however, that looking at the roles of leader and manager separately clarifies two complementary but distinct lines of thinking that contribute to teacher and student success.

My coauthor for this book is Marcia Imbeau, a good friend, colleague, and stellar mentor for novice teachers. Her own teaching experience is as rooted in the elementary classroom as mine is rooted in the secondary classroom. We both know that the principles of managing and leading an effectively differentiated classroom are the same across grades and subjects, but we also know that teachers want and need to see illustrations that match their teaching assignments. We have tried to provide authentic and tested examples of the principles at work in varied grade levels and in varied subjects.

In addition, we both know there is no recipe for effective leadership and management in a differentiated classroom. We don't pretend to provide one. Our goal is to think aloud from the principles that govern our experiences and invite you to think along with us to discover ways to expand your capacity as a teacher who works tirelessly to make room for each student.

For us, this is an "aspirational guide." We have no illusions that any teacher—even the best among us—reads a book and emerges with a radically different teaching style in tow. We do believe, however, that there are many teachers who aspire to grow as professionals every day. We believe there are teachers who will read and reread ideas in pursuit of understanding and insight. We believe there are teachers who, despite powerful forces to the contrary, will act with professional integrity in their classrooms and realize both deeply held and emerging beliefs to benefit each of their students. We believe those teachers exist because we have been taught by them and watched them teach. We've written this book for those aspirational teachers who mean to change themselves and their students—and do.

This new edition of *Leading and Managing a Differentiated Classroom* is based on more than a decade of new research that has evolved since the first edition was published in 2010. It provides readers not only with updated citations but also with narration and examples that derive from that research. It also reflects the continuing development of our thinking about what characterizes effective learner-centered classrooms, based both on research and ongoing experience in our own classrooms as well as in the classrooms and schools across the United States and internationally. In addition, the second edition contains an expanded discussion of approaches that honor and support the diversity of learners in contemporary classroom and uses modified language with a focus on the inclusion of all students in effective differentiation. Our intention here, as in all of our work, is to help build a foundation from which educators can create learning environments and opportunities appropriate to their own particular and unique contexts. Thanks for thinking along with us!

Carol Tomlinson

Part I

Leading for a Differentiated Classroom

The teacher's overriding moral purpose is to meet the needs of students, even when it conflicts with personal preferences.

—Lorna Earl, *Assessment as Learning*

A chorus of voices—representative of experts in virtually every aspect of education—continually asserts that current ideas about "how to do school" are inadequate, both as a reflection of our current knowledge of teaching and learning *and* as a means to address the learning needs of an increasingly diverse student population. In terms of incorporating contemporary knowledge of how people learn into the classroom, experts make the analogy that we're settling for a Model T Ford instead of drawing on 21st century automotive engineering.

New Expectations to Meet the Needs of a New Generation of Learners

More to the point, the old images of effective classrooms are anachronistic in terms of today's students and their needs. Not only do learners in our schools compose an increasingly diverse group, but they are also young people who live in a world of personalization, at least outside school. They watch the entertainment they want on demand rather than on some network programmer's schedule. They order custom computers that are specifically equipped for their needs and desires. They get news on demand and the information they need, when they need it. In school, however, they're often still taught as though their variance in readiness, individual interests, and particular approaches to learning are of no consequence. It is becoming increasingly difficult to pretend that batch processing of a vastly diverse student population supports them as learners or that we are preparing them for productive citizenship in a world with complexities, uncertainties, and challenges that demand the very best from each of them.

Consider the following sets of excerpts from documents published by five key education organizations in the United States. Together, they provide a comprehensive look at the expectations for teachers in today's classrooms—what's necessary to work effectively with a broad range of learners and the spectrum of strengths and needs those learners bring with them into the classroom.

Some general expectations for teachers

The first set of excerpts comes from the Interstate Teacher Assessment and Support Consortium (InTASC), an organization that publishes standards reflecting professional consensus about what teachers should know and be able to do, regardless of their specialty areas.

The surge in learner diversity means teachers need knowledge and skills to customize learning for learners with a range of individual differences. These differences include students who have disabilities and students who perform above grade level and deserve opportunities to accelerate. Differences also include cultural and linguistic diversity and the specific needs of students for whom English is a new language. Teachers need to recognize that all learners bring to their learning varying experiences, abilities, talents, and prior learning, as well as language, culture, and family and community values that are assets that can be used to promote their learning. To do this effectively, teachers must have a deeper understanding of their own frames of reference (e.g., culture, gender, language, abilities, ways of knowing), the potential biases in these frames, and their impact on expectations for and relationships with learners and their fami-lies. Finally, teachers need to provide multiple approaches to learning for each student. (Council of Chief State School Officers [CCSSO], 2013, p. 4)

Teaching begins with the learner. To ensure that each student learns new knowledge and skills, teachers must understand that learning and develop-mental patterns vary among individuals, that learners bring unique individual differences to the learning process, and that learners need supportive and safe learning environments to thrive. Effective teachers have high expectations for each and every learner and implement developmentally appropriate, challeng-ing learning experiences within a variety of learning environments that help all learners meet high standards and reach their full potential. Teachers do this by combining a base of professional knowledge, including an understanding of how cognitive, linguistic, social, emotional, and physical development occurs, with the recognition that learners are individuals who bring differing personal and family backgrounds, skills, abilities, perspectives, talents and interests. Teachers collaborate with learners, colleagues, school leaders, families, members of the learners' communities, and community organizations to better understand their students and maximize their learning. Teachers promote learners' acceptance of responsibility for their own learning and collaborate with them to ensure the effective design and implementation of both self-directed and collaborative learning.

- **Standard #1: Learner Development.** The teacher understands how learners grow and develop, recognizing that patterns of learning and devel-opment vary individually within and across the cognitive, linguistic, social, emotional, and physical areas, and designs and implements developmen-tally appropriate and challenging learning experiences.
- **Standard #2: Learning Differences.** The teacher uses understanding of individual differences and diverse cultures and communities to ensure inclusive learning environments that enable each learner to meet high standards.
- **Standard #3: Learning Environments.** The teacher works with others to create environments that support individual and collaborative learning, and that encourage positive social interaction, active engagement in learn-ing, and self-motivation. (CCSSO, 2013, p. 8)

Some expectations for "accomplished" teachers

The second set of excerpts comes from the National Board for Professional Teaching Standards (NBPTS)—the body that provides the framework for National Board certification of "accomplished" teachers in the United States.

The National Board provides standards in most content areas that describe the attributes of such teachers. Written by teachers, the standards guide the rigorous requirements for receiving National Board certification. While the standards in each content area reflect the nature and processes of that discipline, standards in *all* content areas assert that accomplished teachers prioritize the following:

- Knowing students as individuals.
- Creating a learning environment in which the varied cultures, experiences, strengths, needs, and pathways to learning of every learner in the class are respected.
- Using curriculum that reflects the principles and practices of the discipline and emphasizes student engagement and understanding.
- Employing persistent formative assessment to understand the development of individual students in critical knowledge, understanding, and skills.
- Using formative assessment information to plan instruction that meets the varied student needs, strengths, and interests that exist in all classrooms, and to help students develop agency as learners.
- Planning instruction that is guided by formative assessment and that enables every student to work successfully with problem solving, collaboration, developing meaningful products for meaningful audiences, and mirroring the work of experts in the discipline.
- Creating and leading classrooms that use time, space, materials, and other elements to consistently address the needs of both individual students and the class as a whole.

Although these principles form the architecture of effective differentiation and accurately describe "accomplished" teachers, the authors of the National Board did not "borrow" the underpinnings of differentiation any more than differentiation "borrowed" the language of the National Board standards. Rather, both draw on our current best knowledge of teaching and learning and simply commend to educators the value of using that knowledge to guide our work every day, throughout a career, with the goal of maximizing the learning of every student in our care.

Here are a few representative examples of National Board standards in language arts and mathematics.

Accomplished English language arts teachers use their knowledge of students to strategically match the best instructional practice with individual students or groups of students, differentiating support as needed to foster students' literacy development. Accomplished teachers adjust the curriculum to match the student in ways that promote learning within each student's optimal range of development. [They] know that targeting instruction that is challenging to a student while being sensitive to his or her developmental level enhances the potential for student engagement with learning and fosters growth…and do not assume that students share the same background or aspirations. Accomplished English language arts teachers are adept at creating assignments that build on individuality, and they provide students with opportunities to read, view, write, and produce varied types of texts about topics that interest them. Teachers also can help students develop knowledge and skills in areas in which they might not currently have an interest, skillfully creating engagement with subjects that might otherwise provoke boredom or resistance. Accomplished teachers ensure that every student has the opportunity for their individual voice to be heard. (NBPTS, 2014, pp. 23–24)

Accomplished English language arts teachers understand that the equitable treatment of students may sometimes involve treating students differently. To be fair and equitable, teachers must know their students' needs and consider each student individually. This consideration means that teachers play to their students' strengths and provide extra support when needed, allowing students differentiated opportunities to demonstrate their knowledge and skills. Accomplished teachers deliberately seek out paths that will provide insights into their students' [strengths and needs] and then they connect this information to their instructional decision making. Teachers sensitively frame the way they approach a lesson, a piece of literature, or a classroom discussion using detailed knowledge of students' diverse outlooks and backgrounds.

Accomplished English language arts teachers recognize that students come to the classroom with prior experiences and perspectives that both differentiate them from and connect them with their peers. Accomplished teachers are well attuned to this variety and guide students to create classroom norms that address, accept, and celebrate these differences and similarities. Moreover, accomplished teachers understand the many ways students seek to distinguish themselves from their peers. They monitor and respond appropriately with strategies that will not only advance student learning, but also improve understanding among students and foster a shared sense of community. (NBPTS, 2014, pp. 28–29)

Accomplished teachers take into account the individual needs and developmental levels of students when designing instruction. Teachers know how to observe and listen to students' interactions in order to blend instructional goals for the lesson with the learning goals of students. Teachers constantly reflect on the interaction between the purpose of the lesson and the requirements of the student to effectively satisfy both. Teachers use these observations to differentiate their instruction by providing different entry points to the same assignment with different skill sets. (NBPTS, 2010, p. 33)

Accomplished teachers value mathematics. They take joy in it. They appreciate how knowledge in mathematics is created. They are excited by the ideas they explore with students. Teachers communicate that joy to their students. Teachers use the power of mathematics to fascinate students. Teachers elicit mathematical excitement and provide students with opportunities to experience the intellectual satisfaction that comes from finding a solution to a problem or justifying a conjecture. Instead of simply telling students how to solve a problem, the teacher may scaffold activities to help students recognize and celebrate their ability to use their knowledge of mathematics to answer questions. (NBPTS, 2010, p. 35)

The look of the classroom of an accomplished [mathematics] teacher also tells something about the role mathematics plays in students' everyday lives in school. Student work, mathematical models, and manipulative materials likely to pique students' interests and encourage their involvement in mathematics are evident in these teachers' classrooms. The physical arrangement of space and furniture, along with teachers' use of space, is purposeful and designed to foster mathematical discourse and support both collaborative and independent student work. Teachers working in circumstances in which they have little or no control over their physical setting make whatever accommodations they can to contribute to students' learning in and thinking about mathematics. (NBPTS, 2010, p. 37)

Accomplished teachers view ongoing assessment as an integral part of their instruction, benefitting both the teacher and the student. Teachers—guided by well-defined instructional goals of the current class and students' future mathematical classes—design appropriate assessments and activities to monitor the progress of the class as a whole, as well as the work of individual students. Mathematics teachers skillfully incorporate opportunities for assessing students' progress into daily instruction. Using levels and types of questioning, teachers assess students' abilities to comprehend, apply, and synthesize. Teachers use a variety of strategies to explore and expand their students' thinking and a variety of methods to check for students' understanding, and teachers use this information to shape their teaching. Throughout the assessment process, teachers monitor the skills that students may be missing and find ways to design or modify instruction to minimize gaps in learning. (NBPTS, 2010, p. 41)

More expectations for all teachers

The other excerpts we want to share come from the National Association for the Education of Young Children (NAEYC), the Association for Middle Level Education (AMLE), and the National Association of Secondary School Principals (NASSP). Together, these three organizations cover the full sweep of professional expectations for teachers—from novice to expert, preschool level through high school—and their message is clear and consistent: student differences matter, and effective teachers attend to those differences thoughtfully, proactively, in ways that reflect quality practice in all aspects of teaching and for all learners, and with firm intent to open the way for each learner to have equity of access to excellent learning opportunities.

Let's begin with some recommendations for early childhood educators set by NAEYC:

- **Uphold the unique value and dignity of each child and family.** Ensure that all children see themselves and their daily experiences, as well as the daily lives of others within and beyond their community, positively reflected in the design and implementation of pedagogy, curriculum, learning environment, interactions, and materials. Celebrate diversity by acknowledging similarities and differences and provide perspectives that recognize beauty and value across differences.

- **Recognize each child's unique strengths and support the full inclusion of all children—given differences in culture, family structure, language, racial identity, gender, abilities and disabilities, religious beliefs, or economic class.** Help children get to know, recognize, and support one another as valued members of the community. Take care that no one feels bullied, invisible, or unnoticed.

- **Develop trusting relationships with children and nurture relationships among them while building on their knowledge and skills.** Embrace children's cultural experiences and the languages and customs that shape their learning. Treat each child with respect. Eliminate language or behavior that is stereotypical, demeaning, exclusionary, or judgmental.

- **Consider the developmental, cultural, and linguistic appropriateness of the learning environment and your teaching practices for each child.** Offer meaningful, relevant, and appropriately challenging activities across all interests and abilities. Children of all genders, with and without disabilities, should see themselves and their families, languages, and cultures regularly and meaningfully reflected in the environment and learning materials. Counter common stereotypes and misinformation. Remember that the learning environment and its materials reflect what you do and do not value by what is present and what is omitted. (NAEYC, 2019, p. 7)

Further, NAEYC advocates that teachers do the following:

• **Use their knowledge of each child and family to make learning experiences meaningful, accessible, and responsive to each and every child.** Building on the relationships they nurture with each child and family and between children…educators design learning activities that reflect the lives and cultures of each child. (2020, p. 21)

• **[Be] prepared to individualize their teaching strategies to meet the specific needs of individual children, including children with disabilities and children whose learning is advanced, by building upon their interests, knowledge, and skills.** (2020, p. 22)

• **Actively promote children's agency. Provide each child with opportunities for rich, engaging play and opportunities to make choices in planning and carrying out activities.** Use open-ended activities that encourage children to work together and solve problems to support learning across all areas of development and curriculum. (2019, p. 7)

In *The Successful Middle School: This We Believe,* AMLE asserts the following:

Challenging curriculum addresses substantive concepts and skills and is appropriately geared to each student's level of understanding and readiness.… Attuned to the vast developmental and identity-related diversity of their learners, middle school teachers know students' prior experiences, social and cultural backgrounds, and learning preferences. This knowledge, along with thoughtful use of formative and summative assessment data, informs curriculum. In successful middle schools, learning tasks are perceived as achievable, even if difficult, and reflect high expectations for all students. (Bishop & Harrison, 2021, p. 47)

Expecting students to grapple with and master advanced concepts requires middle grades teachers to stretch themselves well beyond "covering material." … Using their professional judgment and in consultation with students, teachers guide the selection of ideas and concepts for in-depth study. To help these issues come alive, teachers invite students to examine values, assumptions, basic principles, and alternative points of view, addressing why things happen as well as how. Students learn skills and concepts as they become explorers, thinkers, and communicators. (Bishop & Harrison, 2021, p. 46)

Learning in middle schools can be complex, messy, and wonderful, as students regularly set personal goals, chart their growth, work independently and collaboratively, and reflect on their progress. The wide variety of teaching approaches, the personalization of learning opportunities, and the presence of integrative curriculum call for assessment practices that are equally varied. Evidence of middle grades learning can be demonstrated in many ways, including presentations, performances, portfolios, projects, journals, artwork, teacher and peer feedback, teacher-designed tests, and audio or video documentation. (Bishop & Harrison, 2021, p. 61)

Finally, NASSP makes the following points in its 2018 publication *Building Ranks: A Comprehensive Framework for Effective School Leaders*:

- School leaders guarantee that each person is known, valued, treated justly, and receives the individualized, high-quality education necessary to succeed in a global society. (p. 46)
- Although the focus is often on addressing the needs of students who are struggling, it's important to ensure that each student—high-performing, low-performing, and in-between—has access to the supports he or she needs to be successful. (p. 62)
- Schools were historically designed to "teach to the middle." You [the principal] have the responsibility to shift the mindsets and practices that target the majority of students to ones that address the learning, physical, and social-emotional needs of each student. (p. 60)
- Expectations should be high for each person and void of biases associated with an individual's background… [and] tailor the growth opportunities to the specific needs of each student… to maximize his or her personal development and academic… learning. When leaders individually address each person's learning needs, they maximize growth. (p. 84)
- Ensuring that each student is known and feels he or she is part of the learning community is the foundational element of equity. Without knowing each of your students, you can't be certain that each one is receiving equitable treatment. Nor can you identify supports to meet each student's full range of needs. (pp. 85–86)
- Relationships enable learning by fostering a sense of belonging as well as a commitment to shared goals. When students have strong relationships with one another and with staff members, they are more committed to their education and more engaged in their learning…. Strong relationships are characterized by trust, communication, mutual respect, and support. (p. 100)
- Curriculum, instruction, and assessments… should be aligned to high expectations for student learning…. intellectually challenging, anchored in authentic learning experiences, and strengths-based. (p. 100)

• Differentiated and personalized quality curriculum, instruction, and assess-ments also regularly check for student understanding within lessons and use interim and summative assessments to track student progress. Data produced by those various assessments inform continuous adaptations and improvement. (p. 204)

Despite consistent and often urgent calls for teachers to attend to individual learners' needs, and in spite of daily evidence that one-size-fits-all instruction fails many if not most students, it is extraordinarily difficult for us to pull away from antiquated conceptions and embrace more contemporary and effective ways of thinking about teaching and learning.

There are many reasons the idea of teaching with the individual in mind is challenging (if not confounding), not the least of which are classroom images that are indelible in the minds of teachers, students, and parents alike. These familiar images and impressions have become second nature to so many of us because they are continually reinforced throughout our young lives. We all think we know the right way "to do school." Even very young children who play school at home know the rules: The "teacher" is in charge and the "students" sit silently in straight rows and watch the teacher, who tells the students what to learn. Students learn what they're told and repeat it back to the teacher. The teacher teaches everyone alike (which is only fair), and students who can't fol-low the rules or get restless with the routine get booted "out of class." Students who cannot keep up with the schedule of "coverage," or otherwise fall behind, are regularly placed into low-track groups or classes and taught by teachers who are often less experienced or less well-prepared for the work they need to do than are teachers assigned high-track classes. We generally accept that in low-track classes, teachers must "teach down" to students in order to "meet them where they are academically," even though this practice often leads to students falling even further behind more educationally advantaged students, whose academic fare is considerably more likely to prepare them for the world in which they will lead (Berwick, 2019; Lieberman, 2020; Truong, 2022).

While this description may sound like a caricature of an actual classroom, it represents a set of beliefs about teaching and learning that are deeply embedded in most people. Whether we are teachers, parents, or students, these beliefs are a common set of blueprints for thinking about the right way to "do school"; it is difficult to conceive of the classroom in any other way. Nevertheless, if we aspire to teach so that each of our students is prepared to assume meaningful and sat-isfying roles in a world that is quite different from the factory-based era that the current model of schooling was designed to serve, learner-focused change is not an option but an imperative.

Classroom Teachers as Leaders for Change

Responsibility for supporting change toward student-focused instruction belongs to many kinds of educators. Superintendents, principals, curriculum coordinators, specialists, grade-level coordinators, department chairs, media directors, and counselors are some of the educational players who have pivotal roles to play in recrafting classrooms so that they more effectively teach the diverse learners who populate them. This job is vastly easier when everyone works as a team toward a shared goal, and it is unacceptable for anyone in the chain to abdicate their responsibility to make school "work" for each and every student there. Nonetheless, the role of the classroom teacher in bringing about such change is central. No one else is as vital. If every other educator fails to assume the responsibility of leadership for student-focused change, the classroom teacher still has the power to re-envision and reinvent teaching and learning.

It is the classroom teacher who has an unspoken contract with each learner to make productive use of time spent in the classroom. It is the classroom teacher who is in a unique position to see beyond multilayered distractions and disguises to know each learner as an individual human being. It is the classroom teacher who identifies or creates the links that exist between each individual learner and the critical content. It is the classroom teacher who taps into hidden motivations, builds bridges to span damaged trust, and reveals to each student how the learning process makes us fully human. Quite simply, the classroom teacher is an irreplaceable leader in moving differentiation from an abstract idea on paper or in a professional development session to a fundamental way of life in the classroom.

This book will highlight four different audiences for whom teacher leadership is essential to make student-focused instruction a reality. First, teachers must do the daily work of motivating *themselves* to plan and implement instruction that keeps students in the foreground and of primary concern. Second, teachers must motivate, lead, and direct *students* to understand, contribute to, and participate in a classroom that is designed to take into account the needs of individuals and the group. Third, teachers need to lead *parents* to understand the goals of a student-focused or responsive classroom, how those goals will benefit their children, and how they can contribute to the success of their children and of the classroom. Finally, teachers can be important leaders for *other teachers* and for *school administrators* in understanding and contributing intelligently to academically responsive instruction. This audience is of particular note, since teachers often don't see themselves as leaders of school leaders, but that role is just as important as the other three. Strong, informed, mission-driven leadership from school administrators—particularly a school's principal—is necessary for the kind and degree of support needed for schoolwide change. Teachers who communicate their hopes, aspirations, successes, and struggles to designated school leaders can be a powerful and convincing source of information and motivation for principals and other school leaders who want to expand their efforts beyond meeting the demands of daily school operations.

Successful teachers are natural leaders. Along the way, we manage the details necessary to achieve goals that we have every reason to believe will benefit those who follow us. Genuine leadership indicates an ethical orientation—one that merits the trust of followers. To achieve such a level of leadership, we must do the following:

- Work from and aspire to practices that are an evident improvement over the status quo.
- Articulate a vision for change so that those who are asked to follow the vision have a compelling reason to do so.
- Move knowledgeably toward this vision while simultaneously attending to the voices and needs of those who will necessarily help enact it.
- Be patient with and supportive of those we lead yet impatient with artificial barriers to progress.
- Maintain a pace that consistently ensures visible progress without pushing the system beyond its capacity to change.
- Monitor outcomes of the change and be willing to adapt, when necessary, to achieve desirable outcomes and eliminate undesirable outcomes.

Teacher Leadership for Differentiated Classrooms

The three chapters in Part I of this book are designed to help teachers be more confident and effective leaders *for* and *in* student-focused/responsive/differentiated classrooms. We do not presume that these chapters contain all there is to know about the topics they address; each chapter provides, at best, an overview of a much more complex issue. We also know that individuals who invest their energies in any approach continue to transform and augment that approach. Our goal, then, is not to present the final word in regard to teacher leadership for differentiation but rather to offer a framework for an intelligent beginning.

In our experience, teachers who are most effective with differentiation operate from strong (and growing) knowledge bases that are rooted in a philosophy of what classrooms could be like if they maximized the capacity of each learner. These teachers invite learners to help them construct such a classroom and to attend to its health as the academic year progresses. For these teachers, differentiation is not a set of strategies but rather a demographically necessary, ethically focused, pedagogically informed, and empirically tested way of thinking about the work they do.

Effective teacher leaders are knowledgeable about and continue to nurture their knowledge of the areas in which they seek to lead. Chapter 1 reviews the elements of differentiated instruction for teachers who want to lead toward differentiation. Effective leaders work from a philosophy or belief system that informs the vision they commend to others. Chapter 2 articulates the philosophy that undergirds what we call "differentiation" so that teachers who seek to lead toward differentiation are grounded in their own views on teaching. Leaders engage followers in understanding and contributing to a shared vision. Chapter 3 provides suggestions for talking with students, parents, and other educators about differentiation so that teacher leaders can confidently invite them to participate in creating a place and processes that benefit the broadest possible array of learners.

1

Understanding Differentiation in Order to Lead
Aiming for Fidelity to a Model

Few would argue that opportunity in life is strongly connected with educational opportunity. However, we have often misconstrued the notion of equal access to education to mean that all students should receive precisely the same pacing, resources, and instruction. The result is a one-size-fits-all education system. Differentiated instruction recognizes that students are not the same and that access to equal education necessarily means that, given a certain goal, each student should be provided resources, instruction, and support to help them meet that objective.

—John Stroup, University of Virginia doctoral student

"My district wanted all of its teachers to differentiate instruction," a young woman told me. "So they created a notebook of differentiation strategies for us. It's really nice—bound and everything. I guess it must have a dozen strategies in it."

"I'm glad you found it useful," I responded.

She paused, searching for a reply. "I did find it useful," she said. "I used every one of the ideas. And now I guess I'm just waiting for the next notebook."

This young teacher was puzzled. Having now "done differentiation" cover to cover, she seemingly had no idea where to go next. Without an understanding of how the ideas in the notebook had been generated, she had no basis for taking the next steps. I was reminded of Ralph Waldo Emerson's caution that if we only learn methods, we are tied to those methods, but if we learn principles, we can develop our own methods.

My conversation with this young teacher reflected several common misunderstandings about differentiation:

Misunderstanding: Differentiation is a set of instructional strategies.

Reality: Differentiation is a philosophy—a way of thinking about teaching and learning. It is a set of principles that, once adopted, can become a way of being in the classroom.

Misunderstanding: It's adequate for a district or school leader (or professional developers) to tell, or even show, teachers how to differentiate instruction effectively.

Reality: Learning to differentiate instruction well requires rethinking one's classroom practice and results from an ongoing process of trial, reflection, and adjustment in the classroom itself.

Misunderstanding: Differentiation is something a teacher does or doesn't do (as in, "I already do that" or "I tell our teachers that they already differentiate instruction").

Reality: Most teachers who remain in a classroom for longer than a day *do* pay attention to student variation and respond to it in some way—especially with students who can jeopardize order in the classroom. However, very few teachers proactively plan instruction to consistently address student differences in readiness, interest, and learning preferences based on ongoing assessment insights, including focused classroom observation and conversations with students.

Misunderstanding: Differentiation is just about instruction.

Reality: Although differentiation is an instructional approach, effective differentiated instruction is inseparable from a positive learning environment, high-quality curriculum, assessment that informs teacher and student decision making, and student–teacher partnerships to develop and use flexible classroom routines. To the degree that any one of those elements is weak, the others are also diminished—and student growth is diminished as well.

The purpose of this chapter is to provide a brief summary of what we call *differentiated instruction*; you can find a full explanation of the elements of this approach in other resources (e.g., Sousa & Tomlinson, 2018; Tomlinson, 2014, 2017, 2021, 2022; Tomlinson & McTighe, 2006; Tomlinson & Moon, 2013; Tomlinson & Murphy, 2015). A clear understanding of the individual elements of differentiation and how they relate to and shape the classroom system paves the way for a more robust exploration of the philosophy of differentiation, which directs how teachers manage and lead an effectively differentiated classroom.

What's important to understand before reading on is that the core intent of differentiation is to help teachers place *the* student, singular, at the center of all classroom decisions—not the *students,* plural (as though they were a single, uniform entity); not a standardized test; not "content coverage"; and not technology or texts or time or space—and to do so with the goal of enabling every student to access genuinely excellent curriculum, instruction, assessment practices, and human support. Working diligently toward those things constitutes fidelity to the concept of differentiation.

The guidelines we provide in this book for accomplishing those goals reflect our best understanding of each of the classroom elements as well as what it means to honor each learner and distinguish our profession. We cannot offer a foolproof recipe for effective differentiation, but we can provide guidance and counsel in the form of proven principles and practices that can help you grow in understanding and application of differentiation's core intent. We also know that your work will be enhanced and extended as you more fully understand your students' strengths and needs and as you amplify the model of differentiation with your own creativity and problem-solving skills.

Key Elements of Differentiated Instruction

Differentiation can be accurately described as classroom practice with a balanced emphasis on individual students and the class as a whole. In other words, in an effectively differentiated classroom, it is understood that

- Students differ as learners in terms of background experience, culture, race, language, gender expression, strengths, interests, readiness to learn, modes of learning, speed of learning, support systems for learning, self-awareness as a learner, confidence as a learner, independence as a learner, learning exceptionality, and a host of other ways.

• Differences profoundly affect how students learn and the nature of scaffolding they will need at various points in the learning process.

• Teachers have a responsibility to ensure that each of their students masters the most important ideas, processes, and skills in the disciplines they study.

• Teachers make specific and continually evolving plans to connect each learner with that essential content.

• Teachers work persistently to understand the experiences, strengths, and needs of each of their students, in addition to the nature of the content they teach.

• The goal in a differentiated classroom is to support each learner's access to high-quality curriculum, instruction that inspires learning, and the support necessary to succeed.

• A flexible approach to teaching and learning "makes room" for student variance.

• Teachers continually ask, "What does *this* student need at *this* moment in order to be able to progress with *this* key content—and what do *I* need to do to make that happen?"

At the core of the classroom practice of differentiation is the modification of four curriculum-related elements—*content, process, product,* and *affect*—which are based on three categories of student need and variance—*readiness, interest,* and *learning preferences.*

Content

The knowledge, understanding, and skills we ask students to learn—or how students access that knowledge, understanding, and skill.

In differentiation, we emphasize varied methods or modes that students can use to access key content (e.g., text at varied levels of complexity, recorded text, podcasts, videos, images, graphics, apps, websites with working models, interviews, demonstrations, small-group instruction, and so on) rather than change the content itself (Tomlinson, 2021, 2022; Tomlinson & McTighe, 2006). There are instances, however, when some students need to go back to prerequisite content in order to move ahead, when advanced learners need to move ahead before their classmates are ready to do so, when students would benefit from interest-focused investigations, and when student individualized education programs (IEPs) direct the teacher to change the content itself.

Process

How students come to understand or make sense of the content.

Real learning—the sort that enables students to retain, apply, and transfer content—happens *in* students, not *to* them (National Research Council, 2000; Tomlinson, 2021, 2022; Wiggins & McTighe, 2005). The word *process* is often used as a synonym for *activities*. However, activities can be misaligned with content goals; fail to require students to think through, grapple with, or use essential knowledge, understanding, and skills; and even be mind-numbingly tedious. Therefore, it is wise to substitute the term *sense-making activities* to emphasize that what we ask students to do in the name of learning should most often help them to "own" the content, see how it makes sense, realize how it connects with their lives, understand how it is useful in the world outside the classroom, examine varied perspectives on it, address issues and solve problems using it, role-play it, debate it, represent it graphically, and so on.

Product

How students demonstrate what they have come to know, understand, and be able to do after an extended period of learning.

A product is not something students generate in a single lesson or as a result of an activity or two. Rather, it is a rich culminating, authentic assessment that calls on students to apply, extend, or transfer what they have learned over a period of time. Tests can reflect these characteristics when they present students with complex problems to solve or issues to address in ways that require understanding of key ideas, transfer of knowledge, and application of skills. Effectively designed performance assessments inevitably have these characteristics (McTighe et al., 2020; Tomlinson, 2021; Tomlinson & Moon, 2013).

Affect

How students' emotions and feelings impact their learning.

Emotions and feelings originate in the brain based on past experiences and reactions to current experiences. They impact our motivation to learn, ability to work with others, and self-concept as a learner. In that way, affect is integral to, rather than apart from, curriculum and instruction. When a student has a positive affect regarding learning and themselves as a learner, it opens the door to academic growth. Conversely, a student's negative affect regarding learning or their own abilities as a learner effectively shuts the door to learning (Sousa & Tomlinson, 2018). The most effective teachers don't just observe student behavior; they work to understand the affect or emotion that drives behavior so they can guide and support students in a positive direction and help them develop confidence and agency as learners and as people (Tomlinson, 2021, 2022).

Readiness

A student's current proximity to specified knowledge, understanding, and skills.

Readiness is *not* a synonym for *ability*, and the two terms should not be used interchangeably. The term *ability* connotes what we sometimes believe to be a more or less fixed and inborn trait. *Readiness* suggests a temporary condition; it fluctuates in response to curricular changes and high-quality teaching. You'll see, as this chapter continues, that thinking in terms of "student readiness" rather than "student ability" is beneficial to both student and teacher. To grow academically, students must work consistently with tasks that focus on essential knowledge, understanding, and skills and that are a bit too difficult for their current level of proficiency with that content. In addition, students must have a support system in the form of peers and teachers who will help them surmount this difficulty and emerge from the task (or sequence of tasks) at a new and more advanced level of readiness (Sousa & Tomlinson, 2018; Vygotsky, 1978, 1986). Further, teachers who believe in each student's capacity to learn more than the student may believe themselves capable of and who vigorously support each learner's forward progress are likely to have students who come to believe in their own worth as learners and, therefore, become more engaged and successful learners (Dweck, 2006, 2017). In differentiating for student readiness, then, a teacher uses careful formative assessment and classroom observation to understand each student's individual learning trajectory relative to knowledge, understanding, and skills that are critical to mastering current content. Then the teacher provides assignments, timelines, materials, and support systems that enable the learner to grow steadily in proficiency.

Interest

That which engages the attention, curiosity, and involvement of a student.

Student interest is tied directly to student motivation to learn and to learning itself. When student interest is high, motivation to learn is heightened, and learning is enhanced. Working with areas of personal interest helps students try harder, persist longer, think more clearly, understand more deeply, process information more efficiently, and remember more accurately. Interest has the power to transform struggling performers and lift high achievers to a new plane. Personal interests are typically linked to a student's strengths, cultural context, personal experiences, questions, or sense of need (Collins & Amabile, 1999; Csikszentmihalyi, 1990; Paul, 2013).

Learning preferences

An inclination to take in, explore, and express content at a given time and in a given context.

Giving students choices as to how they will take in, make sense of, and express learning is also an important aspect of differentiation. Offering these choices signals to students that the teacher trusts them to make beneficial choices while also helping them be more metacognitive about their own learning. Learning preference options can also increase student ownership of learning and promote the development of both individual voice and decision-making prowess (Dack & Tomlinson, 2015; Draeger & Wilson, 2016).

Noted psychologist and educator Jerome Bruner (1996) wrote that agency presupposes choice. Thus, when learner-centered teachers elicit student voice in what will be learned and how—when, for example, they provide choice of topic or focus for an assignment, mode of learning, or mode of expressing learning—they are likely helping the young people they teach become more independent. After all, the process of achieving agency includes learning to plan for and make *fruitful* decisions. Thus, teachers help students consider what it means to choose a learning path wisely in light of one's goals, strengths, interests, and context by guiding them to consider questions like these:

- How do I decide what my options are?
- How can I monitor my progress as I'm working?
- How can I think about ways in which varied choices will support (or diminish) outcomes that I value?
- How can I recognize when a learning path I have chosen is not serving me well?
- How might I weigh and choose from other options that are available to me?

As students learn how to work independently, with a peer, and with a small group of peers, choice of working conditions is a simple way to honor students' learning preferences. For example, a teacher might provide the option of working alone or with a partner; sitting at a desk, table, or on the floor; using earplugs or headsets if conversation is distracting; or reading a story (or other text) or listening to a recording of that text. Options for exploring or expressing learning can include but are certainly not limited to using print, video, and audio sources; writing a paper; creating an animation; building a model; generating a set of graphs; and creating a photo essay, a role-play, a demonstration, an infographic, or a set of storyboards. The idea is not to provide a string of options for every single assignment but rather to suggest a few options that seem to be a match for the nature of the assignment and students' points of development. It's also easy, and often effective, to encourage students to propose additional ways to learn or express learning that were not on your list of choices.

Researchers (e.g., Katz & Assor, 2007) point out that the choices teachers offer need to feel meaningful to the student to produce beneficial outcomes. So, for example, giving students a choice of how to complete an assignment that they find to be irrelevant or redundant will not be as likely to make a difference in their development as giving learners an assignment that they find interesting and appropriately challenging. It may also be productive for the teacher to explain the reasons behind the specific options for an assignment, product, or assessment; to encourage students to present other options; and to ask students to reflect later on whether particular choices were helpful in their learning (Parker et al., 2017).

A teacher in an effectively differentiated classroom seeks to develop increasing insight into students' readiness levels, interests, and learning preferences. The teacher then modifies content, process, product, and affect in order to develop instruction that maximizes each student's opportunity for academic growth. Figure 1.1 (see p. 36) provides specific examples of how this can play out in the classroom for content, process, and product. By contrast, attending to students' affective needs is generally a matter of the teacher adapting the learning environment or working conditions rather than the other three classroom elements.

Differentiation and the Classroom System

Differentiated instruction is a principle-guided method to approach teaching and learning, and it is implemented in the context of a classroom system that contains five interdependent elements: learning environment, curriculum, assessment, instruction, and leading students and managing flexible routines. In all classrooms, there is a learning environment that is shaped by a teacher's beliefs,

Figure 1.1

A Few Examples of Differentiation Based on Student Need

	Readiness	Interest	Learning Preferences
Content	• Materials at varied readability levels • Recorded text • Video • Images, graphics • Spelling and other skills assigned by current student proficiency • Alternate presentation methods • Targeted small-group instruction • Front-loaded vocabulary • Highlighted texts	• Range of reading materials, videos, interviews, etc., that apply key ideas and skills to a variety of real-world situations • Teacher presentations designed to link essential content to student interests	• Varied teaching modes (e.g., verbal, visual, rhythmic, practical demonstrations, role-play) • Video or audio versions of directions and/or presentations for students who learn better with repeated listening or viewing
Process	• Tiered activities • Mini-workshops • Flexible use of time • Learning contracts • Varied homework assignments • RAFT options • Flexible grouping • Small-group instruction • Use of resources written in English learners' home language and/or initial drafts of products written in home language	• Expert groups • Interest centers • Spotlight on individuals from many cultures who make/have made significant contributions to a discipline • Supplementary materials based on student interests • Jigsaws • Independent inquiries • Interest-based application options • RAFT options	• Choice of working conditions (e.g., alone or with a partner, seated or standing, quietly or with conversation) • Tasks designed around real-world applications • RAFT options • Blogs, vlogs, animations, pod-casts, etc., to explore a topic • Voice-to-text apps for writing
Product	• Tiered product assignments • Personal goal setting • Varied resource options • Check-in requirements based on degree of student independence • Providing samples of quality student work at varied levels of complexity	• Teacher use of student interests in designing products and perfor-mance assessments • Options for students to propose alternate products • Design a Day options • Personalized inquiries • Use of a range of technolo-gies for student exploration and expression	• Complex instruction • Varied formats for expressing key content • Varied working arrangements • Varied modes of demonstrat-ing learning (e.g., video, audio, graphic novels, graphic explana-tions of content in varied disci-plines, interviews, photo essays)

experiences, and actions. There is a curriculum, shaped by a teacher's content knowledge, text materials, and local or federal mandates. There is some form of assessment, again shaped by both the teacher and forces external to the teacher.

Finally, all classrooms benefit from instruction that individual teachers design (or follow established designs for) and implement.

The way in which the teacher envisions and enacts each of these elements shapes each of the other elements. For example, an assessment that feels judgmental to students will negatively impact the learning environment. Likewise, a classroom in which curriculum is highly prescribed, with few or no options for a teacher to make professional decisions on behalf of students, limits that teacher's options for instruction. This book focuses on the fifth foundational element in effective differentiation: leading students and working with them to establish and implement classroom routines that allow flexibility in teaching and learning while ensuring stability that is necessary for both.

The particular model of differentiation supported in this book adopts the position that each of these five elements must be shaped and cultivated to provide opportunities for every student to maximize their learning capacity. Only when each of the elements—separately and in conjunction with one another—supports maximum learning for each student is the classroom functioning as it should.

Learning environment

The physical and emotional context in which learning occurs.

The appearance, organization, and structure of a classroom can invite learning with appealing colors, effective displays of student work, spaces for both solitary and collaborative work, easy access to materials and supplies, furniture arrangements that focus attention on peer input rather than largely or solely on the teacher, and visible cues to support quality work. Conversely, a classroom's physical environment can diminish learning by being barren, drab, cramped, teacher-focused, distracting, or limiting (with seating arrangements that isolate students from one another). More significant than this physical climate, however, is the classroom's more intangible emotional climate. Students learn best when they feel safe, respected, involved, challenged, and supported. Thus, a learning environment that invites each student to be a full participant in the classroom—with full support for the journey—is a necessity for robust differentiated instruction.

Effective differentiation—in other words, effective attention to the learning needs of each student—requires a learning environment in which

- The teacher is attuned and responsive to the affective, cognitive, and social needs of learners.

- Students feel safe, both physically and affectively.
- The teacher respects and supports the possibilities inherent in each student.
- Individual differences are accepted as natural and positive.
- Students learn to respect and support one another as learners.
- Each student makes meaningful contributions to the class.
- The teacher and students share in the decision-making process about daily routines and classroom operation.
- Hard work is an expectation.
- Physical arrangements are flexible and support student access to a variety of learning options.
- A range of resources are available and support student access to content.
- Flexible student grouping capitalizes on student strengths and allows effective attention to student weaknesses.

Curriculum

An organized plan to engage learners with important knowledge, understanding, and skills.

A list of standards is not a curriculum. A textbook is not a curriculum either. Rather, both are ingredients—resources necessary for developing a curriculum.

A high-quality curriculum begins with a teacher's sense of the authentic nature of the discipline that the curriculum will represent. It includes a clear delineation of the essential knowledge students should have and the skills they should master as the result of a particular segment of learning (e.g., a year, a unit of study). It includes summative assessment mechanisms for determining student proficiency with designated outcomes that tightly align with those assessments. It includes a carefully planned sequence of lessons or learning experiences that are designed to *engage* students with *essential* content and to ensure student success with the essential knowledge, understanding, and skills (Erickson et al., 2017; Tomlinson, 2021; Tomlinson et al., 2009; Wiggins & McTighe, 2005).

The model of differentiation represented in this book advocates that all students (unless an IEP indicates otherwise) should do the following:

- Work consistently with curriculum that feels meaningful and relevant.
- Work to master the essential knowledge, understanding, and skills in each lesson and unit of study.
- Be expected to understand what they are learning (versus largely recalling/repeating).

• Be expected to think, and be supported as thinkers, as they engage with curriculum.

• Work with respectful tasks (i.e., tasks that are equally interesting and engaging and that promote understanding of and the ability to apply and transfer essential content).

Assessment

A data-gathering and analysis process that identifies the degree to which students have achieved essential outcomes and informs decisions about and planning for instruction.

There are three kinds of assessment, based on purpose: (1) diagnostic assessment (or pre-assessment), which is designed to determine a student's status relative to essential learning outcomes as a unit of study begins; (2) ongoing assessment, which is designed to follow a student's progress in attaining essential outcomes as a unit of study progresses; and (3) summative assessment, which is designed to measure student outcomes as a unit of study ends or at other key points in a unit or year of study. Both diagnostic and ongoing assessment are formative—that is, they are intended primarily to mentor and support student learning rather than to judge student performance.

High-quality assessments, both formative and summative, guide students in understanding essential learning outcomes, their status relative to those outcomes, and ways in which they can work effectively to maximize their growth toward and beyond those outcomes (Earl, 2013; Tomlinson & Moon, 2013; Wiliam, 2011). The model of differentiation this book supports emphasizes the use of

• Diagnostic formative assessment (pre-assessments) to determine individual students' entry points into a unit of study in terms of their readiness, interest, and learning preferences. Diagnostic formative assessment also enables teachers to discover student misunderstandings about the content. This process is essential to planning for student variance. Diagnostic assessment, of course, should never be graded.

• Ongoing formative assessment to measure a student's developing knowledge, understanding, and skills as a unit progresses. This process is essential to a teacher's preparedness to plan for and support students' varied learning strengths and needs. It is also foundational to guiding students in developing the habits of mind and work that enable them to grow into successful learners. This ongoing formative assessment should rarely, if ever, be graded. Its intent is to generate feedback from the teacher that can focus each student on the next steps in their individual learning progression.

- Summative assessment to offer varied modes of expression and scaffolding (based on students' needs in terms of language, time allocation, writing, etc.). This process helps students express as fully as possible what they know, understand, and can do relative to essential outcomes. Summative assessment occurs after students have had considerable time for practice and guidance. Summative assessment is graded.

Instruction

The process of teaching—that is, engaging students with meaningful content so that they develop essential foundational knowledge and skills as well as understanding of how the content works, how it relates to their lives and experiences, and how they can use what they learn beyond a specific classroom.

Instruction is what many people think of when they think about teaching. It is a complex network of approaches to engaging students with critical content in ways that will enable them to apply it. The teacher acts as a metaphorical bridge, helping students connect the knowledge and skills they already possess with content they are currently learning so they can continue developing as learners and human beings. To plan instruction is to craft a "game plan" for developing students' knowledge, understanding, skills, self-awareness, and agency as learners.

The model of differentiation on which this book is based advocates that instruction will

- Align with essential knowledge, understanding, and skills designated as essential for proficiency.
- Call on students to actively make sense of (come to "own") what we ask them to learn.
- Be designed with student differences in mind, including differences in learning, interests, strengths, culture, language, and gender.
- Be flexible in terms of time, materials, support systems, student groupings, instructional modes, and teaching and learning strategies.
- Offer various routes to accomplishing essential learning outcomes.
- Help students develop voice, self-efficacy, and independence as learners.
- Help students develop proficiency in collaborative learning.
- Provide classroom routines that balance student needs for stability and flexibility (Tomlinson, 2014, 2017, 2021, 2022).

Leading and Managing a Flexible Classroom

This element enables teachers, working in tandem with their students, to create classrooms that place students, with their inevitable variability, at the center of decisions about learning environment, curriculum, assessment, and instruction. It supports the elasticity necessary to move away from paradigms rooted in practices and habits that cast all students of a given age as essentially interchangeable as learners so that the needs of the *students* do not eclipse the needs of *the* student.

As you continue reading this book, it will become clearer how teachers who develop competence and confidence in this element of differentiation increase their capacity to address learning environment, curriculum, assessment, and instruction in ways that invite more students to see teachers as their advocates, to see school as a place that values them, to see learning as a human gift, and to see success as something that belongs to them.

The Interdependence of Classroom Elements

It's likely that many of us began our teaching careers without a clear vocabulary to think about the key classroom elements described in this chapter. It's also likely that we didn't fully grasp how each action we take ripples into all corners of the classroom. Over time, and as we became thoughtful and mindful professionals, we gradually developed a general awareness that our mood and energy levels set in motion "weather fronts" that permeate through the day and affect our students. Our weariness settles on students like fog; our joy becomes their excitement. A test that we have made to seem ominous can bring with it a storm cloud that threatens an otherwise hospitable atmosphere. Our capacity to peacefully disarm a crisis with one student makes the overall learning environment seem more secure for all students in it.

As we continue to develop as professionals, we become more cognizant of how the classroom elements interact. For example, we recognize that if a student feels like an outsider in the classroom, that student is unlikely to commit to class discussions, group work, or even individual tasks, and that this unfavorable learning environment negatively affects the students' experience of both curriculum and instruction. Likewise, if assigned work is consistently beyond the current performance of certain students, they will feel unsafe in the classroom and regard the learning environment as negative. The consequence of such impressions? Students giving up on school or themselves over time.

With time and experience, we are able to anticipate such situations and be proactive with specific and precise strategies to avoid them. For example, if we provide diagrams, examples, and images to ensure that students understand a difficult process before they read the relevant material in their texts, even students who typically resist such independent reading will likely feel that they have a better understanding of what they read. Careful instruction, then, improves the likelihood of a positive experience with curriculum. Figure 1.2 represents the Möbius-like interdependence among curriculum, assessment, and instruction—surrounded by aspects of the learning environment.

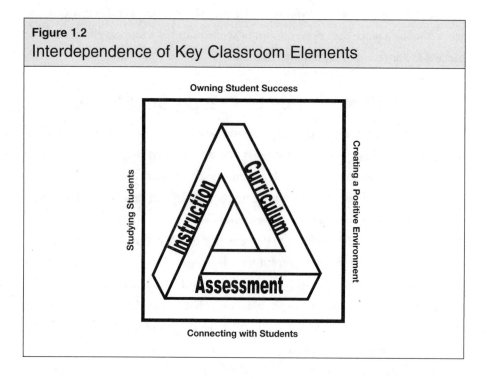

Figure 1.2
Interdependence of Key Classroom Elements

The contents of this chapter represent *what* teachers in successfully differentiated classrooms must create, monitor, and sculpt in order to support the best possible learning outcome for each student. These are the raw materials of teaching. The contents of Chapter 2 examine *why* teachers in effectively differentiated classrooms think about their classrooms in the ways that they do and focuses on the philosophical underpinnings of differentiation. Comfort with both the *what* and the *why* is important in a teacher's ability to lead for differentiation.

2

Teaching What You Believe

A Philosophy to Guide Teachers
Who Lead for Differentiation

When the school bell rings on day one and all our students are in their seats, we will hold the future of this nation and this world in our hands. Whatever we do will have lasting implications, not only on the lives of those students, but also on the lives of all those who they come in contact with. So then, the questions that we should ask ourselves should not be, "How can I make this work?" The question must be, "How can I afford not to make this work?"

—Wendy Kopp, *One Day, All Children*

Few, if any, teachers enter the profession with a well-developed philosophy of teaching. That's something that develops silently, day by day, through crisis and triumph, for those teachers who are willing to risk reflecting on their work and their own role in that work. Experts who study change in a wide variety of fields and over many decades have pondered whether it is more likely for people to believe their way into new actions or act their way into new beliefs. The consensus is the latter. In terms of teacher change, this means that when a teacher tries something new in a classroom and finds it beneficial to students, that action shapes the teacher's beliefs about what works and how an effective classroom proceeds. The "action route" is more likely to result in both teacher growth as a practitioner and positive beliefs about the efficacy of the approach than spending the same amount of time thinking about whether or not to implement it.

If teachers were required to enter their first classroom with the philosophical tenets of differentiation fully in tow, we would have no teachers. Our best hope for classrooms that work effectively for each student is to cultivate teachers who care deeply about teaching and the young people they teach; who believe teaching is a calling, not just a job; and whose firm intent is to become self-actualized professionals who pave the way for their students to also become self-actualized. It is certainly the case that teachers who lead effectively for differentiation operate from a clear sense that classrooms should model a world in which learning is rewarding and in which mutual respect, persistent effort, and shared responsibility make everyone stronger.

It is possible to make a strong case for differentiation simply based on the demographics of contemporary classrooms and the needs of an increasingly diverse student population to function in an increasingly complex world. It is also possible to make a strong case for differentiation based on research (e.g., Tomlinson, 2021, 2022). We believe, however, that the practice of differentiation has its roots in a student-centered philosophy, or ethic, of teaching.

The goal in briefly examining the philosophy behind differentiation in this chapter is not to suggest that educators wait to try to address student learning needs until they have this belief system—or any other—solidly in place. Rather, our hope is that reflecting on these ideas will be beneficial to teachers who want to lead for differentiation, helping them examine their own beliefs and understand some of the thinking that undergirds a coherent, determined, and proactive approach to differentiating instruction. This reflection should also help teachers develop a rationale or vision that will help them talk with their students about a differentiated classroom and make instructional decisions to benefit their students.

There are numerous ways to order the ideas that follow. The method we've chosen seems as logical as any, yet we know that for many teachers, these ideas do not evolve in a logical or even "stepwise" fashion. We are aware, too, that many of these beliefs are interconnected—difficult to separate from one another. We also recognize that we include only a sampling of insights in each area and invite readers to add their thinking to ours.

We'll begin by taking a look at some core tenets of the philosophy of differentiation. Then, we will consider how those beliefs, or principles, might shape a teacher's affective response to students' affective needs. Finally, we'll examine some concrete examples of how those principles might guide teachers' aspirations to establish, lead, and ultimately manage flexible routines in a differentiated classroom.

Beliefs That Point to Differentiated Instruction

Lorna Earl reflects, "Differentiation is making sure that the right students get the right learning tasks at the right time. Once you have a sense of what each student holds as 'given' or 'known' and what he or she needs in order to learn, differentiation is no longer an option. It is an obvious response" (2013, p. 131).

This is an immensely practical way to look at differentiation, but it also models a useful cause-and-effect approach to thinking about the philosophical roots of differentiation. To take some liberties with her words, Earl is in essence saying that if we care about whether teaching and learning are working for each of our students, we must continue to monitor their growth in terms of what we deem to be critical learning goals. Inevitably, we'll find that students are in different places with their mastery of those goals. Then, as she suggests, because we want to make sure each student succeeds, we have no choice but to differentiate instruction so that each learner can take their own next steps forward each day in our classrooms. There's simply no good alternative.

The belief that sets Earl's sequence of thoughts in motion is an affirmation in the profound worth of every learner—not a vague, generalized, mission-statement sort of belief. A belief in the worth of the individual propels a teacher to look "eyeball to eyeball" at the humanity of each student and dictate classroom practice as a result. The statement asks, "If you believe *X*, what choice do you have but *Y*?" Following is a set of beliefs leading to classroom practice that doggedly attend to the needs of individual learners because *there simply is no other choice.*

Belief 1: Every student has inherent dignity and is worthy of respect

At the center of democracy, and the world's major religions, resides a conviction that we should hold human life in esteem and regard it with a sense of awe. From this comes the admonition that each life is unique, irreplaceable, and innately valuable—regardless of race, economic status, language, gender identity, religion, or exceptionality. In most societies, the mature individual is cast as one who can move beyond egocentrism to recognize and address the needs of others and can seek justice not just for oneself but for others. Words affirming human dignity surround us and are prevalent in government documents, houses of worship, judicial rulings, political conversations, and ethical debates. The danger, of course, is that although we generally "accept" the idea of human dignity almost automatically in much of the free world, we enact this idea with much greater difficulty.

The teacher who both accepts and enacts the principle of human dignity does not look at a class roster and simply see a list of names. That teacher considers teaching to be a stewardship of young lives—a shaping of them—and aspires to act and interact in ways that consistently respect and dignify the worth of each student. Such teachers accept the premise that teaching is essentially about building lives (Tomlinson, 2021).

Much of the impetus for differentiated instruction is predicated on the belief that every young life is of ultimate value and should be treated accordingly by adults who have responsibility for shaping those lives. Decisions about classroom rules, curriculum, instruction, student groupings, discipline, grading, and virtually every other aspect of teaching are shaped by the centrality or marginality of this belief in a teacher's thinking. Attempting to enact this belief into classroom practice certainly does not simplify the teacher's role, but it likely does enrich it.

A belief in the dignity and worth of each student leads teachers to ask questions like these:

- How can I gain an understanding of the particular cultures, talents, strengths, interests, needs, burdens, and dreams this student brings to the classroom daily?
- In what ways can I show this student that I unconditionally respect and value them?
- How do I help this student recognize and extend their strengths?

- How can I ensure my own cultural proficiency in order to be the most effective teacher possible for each learner?
- In what ways can I help students see and value the contributions and potential of every other student in the class?
- How can I guide development of a sense of classroom community and collaboration characterized by empathy and respect?

Belief 2: Diversity is both inevitable and positive

A teacher created a poster that hung prominently in the front of her classroom. It read, "Our similarities make us human. Our differences make us individuals." Her conversations and actions with students persistently reaffirmed the words on the wall. She reminded her students that everyone needs kindness and friends. Everyone makes mistakes. Everyone has good days and bad. These are human things. However, Josh's sense of humor is uniquely his. Javier's Latino background means that he knows things others in the class might not, and the class can therefore learn from him. Andrea's perspectives as the oldest child in a large family help her see things in ways that her classmates might not think of.

Through this, the teacher helps her students learn a critical reality: We are a great deal alike as human beings and, in those ways, we share a common bond, yet human beings differ as well. Sometimes those differences separate us, but they don't need to. They should enrich us—and they do, when we are open to them.

A belief that diversity is both normal and positive leads teachers to ask questions like these:

- How do I contribute to my students' awareness of their core similarities and their individuality?
- How do I seek diverse perspectives on issues and topics in our class?
- How do I help students learn to seek and value multiple perspectives on issues and topics?
- How well do I understand my own culture and how it shapes my perspectives and practices as a person and as a teacher?
- How do I ensure that all students' backgrounds, cultures, races, languages, patterns of communication, preferred ways of learning, and traditions are recognized, honored, and represented in our classroom's operation, curriculum, and materials?
- How do I ensure that each student has equity of access to the highest-quality learning opportunities this school can offer?

- How do I create group work that draws on the particular strengths of each of the group's members?
- How do I ensure that every student can make a significant intellectual contribution to the work of the class?

Belief 3: The classroom should mirror the kind of society we want our students to live in and lead

Certainly, we want young people to live in, value, and defend a society that accords respect and dignity to each of its members. We also live in a time when the world is rapidly becoming everyone's backyard. The United States is an amalgam of languages, cultures, races, economic backgrounds, and possibilities. We therefore need classrooms in which students not only accept but expect, learn from, and value diversity. Thus, the first two beliefs that lead to differentiation are tied to this third belief.

Vivian Paley (1993) saw her kindergartners beginning the practice of excluding peers from games and classroom groups. Understanding the long-term liabilities for both the rejected and the rejecter, she posted a new classroom rule: "You can't say you can't play." Over time, she helped her young students debate the fairness of exclusion. Though conducted in the language of 5-year-olds, the conversations initially sounded remarkably like adult rationales for sorting and separating people. In time, her students came to accept the rule, live by it, appreciate it, and defend it. Even at a young age, they found that it was not possible to simultaneously value and exclude a person or a group. They ultimately understood that if "different" meant you had to be somewhere else, then "different" wasn't a good thing. They came to see differences as just part of who they were rather than reasons to suspect or reject one another.

Likewise, it is difficult to make a compelling argument that a school or teacher has deep regard for the value of each individual and accepts diversity as both normal and desirable while designating some students as "able" and others as "less able" for the purpose of sorting them academically. Our long-standing practices of academic segregation are complex and still advocated and practiced by many. They are also antithetical to the core beliefs and practices of differentiation.

With regard to students with learning challenges, Richard Villa and Jacqueline Thousand remind us, "Inclusive education is about... making a commitment to provide each student in the community, each citizen in a democracy, with the inalienable right to belong.... Inclusion is the opposite of segregation and isolation.... Segregated education creates a permanent underclass of students and conveys to those students that they do not measure up, fit in, or belong" (2005, p. 5). The same could be said of students who live in poverty, students whose first language is not English, students who live in foster care, those who experience trauma, those who struggle with gender identity, those who are rightly afraid to go home at the end of the day, and many other "categories" of learners who often find themselves, in one way or another, excluded from robust and challenging curricula, field trips, access to technology, and other opportunities that both indicate and accord student status. To value is to include, not exclude. To honor diversity is to invite it, not shunt it away (Tomlinson, 2022).

The belief that classrooms should mirror the world we hope our students can live in and lead prompts teachers to ask questions like these:

- How do I come to understand my students' diverse backgrounds and needs so that I can draw on them and ensure that students build on them effectively?
- How do my students and I create an inclusive learning environment in which the full range of students learn well together, not just occupy the same space?
- How do I help students create a classroom in which they understand that we all have different entry points into learning yet share a common need to learn?
- How do students come to encourage and support one another's growth?
- How do students learn to affirm and celebrate one another's growth?

Belief 4: Most students can learn most things that are essential to a given area of study

Teacher beliefs about students' capacity to succeed are often buried beneath consciousness. Those beliefs are nonetheless powerful determinants in shaping both teaching and student attitudes about learning.

Carol Dweck, whose research on motivation spans several decades (e.g., 2000, 2006, 2017), tells us that we develop early in life a mindset about what it means to be smart and how we become successful. Her work suggests two options, a fixed mindset or a growth (fluid) mindset. People who develop a fixed mindset conclude that success comes from inborn ability—that is, a person is born smart or they aren't. People who develop a growth mindset reach a different conclusion. They believe that success isn't determined by innate and immutable ability but rather by persistent and informed effort. To put it another way, people work their way to success.

Students with a fixed mindset feel a sense of inevitability when they encounter difficulty in school. For example, students who struggle with school on a regular basis simply conclude that they can't succeed because they are not smart. Likewise, students who are highly able might balk at challenges because they believe smart people shouldn't have to work hard; if they can't handle the challenge with modest effort, then it's an indication that they aren't smart, and that's an idea they can't abide. In either case, students with a fixed mindset have minimal motivation to work hard.

Students with a growth mindset believe that if a skill or task is difficult, they can nonetheless achieve mastery because their continuing effort will win the day. Their motivation to work hard is high because they believe the payoff will be worth their investment.

Teachers with a fixed mindset certainly "teach" all their students, but they do so with a sense that "some kids will get it, and some won't." In a way, these teachers teach without the expectation that every student will learn. They draw conclusions, often unconsciously and often early in a course or grade, about which students are smart and which are not. They then proceed to teach accordingly, remediating some students and enriching or accelerating others.

Teachers with a growth mindset work from the premise that virtually any student can learn anything if the student is willing to work hard and if they have support in that effort, including support in learning to work in ways that characterize successful people. Such teachers aren't interested in labels or past performance; they simply set out to establish an ethic of hard work and to teach students the skills they need to work effectively. Success with essential learning goals for each student is the only acceptable outcome for these teachers.

Not surprisingly, there is an interaction between the mindsets held by both students and teachers. Figure 2.1 illustrates some of the possible interactions and implications.

It is important to note that Dweck finds people can and do change their mindsets. Teachers with growth mindsets regularly help students understand that they have control over their success, thus enabling students with fixed mindsets to begin to operate from a sense of personal agency.

The contribution of a growth mindset to student motivation and achievement is considerable (Aronson et al., 2002; Good et al., 2003; Ng, 2018; O'Keefe et al., 2018; Sparks, 2021). Students who come to believe that their hard work will lead to success earn higher achievement test scores and grades, engage in academics at a higher level, and enjoy the academic process more than students who retain a fixed mindset perspective.

Figure 2.1
Possible Interactions Between Teacher and Student Mindset

		Fixed Mindset (Teacher)	**Growth Mindset** (Teacher)
STUDENT	**Growth Mindset**	Teacher may underestimate student capacity and willingness to work hard and "teach down" because of the student's language, culture, economic status, race, label, etc.	Both teacher and student study student growth, set goals for progress, and look for ways to continue development. Students at all readiness levels have maximum opportunity for challenge, growth, and success.
	Fixed Mindset	Both teacher and student accept the student's difficulties as given, and neither exerts the effort needed for high levels of student achievement. Both also accept high grades on grade-level work as adequate for advanced learners.	Teacher encourages and insists on student effort and growth. Over time, the student's mindset can change to a growth orientation with evidence that effort leads to success. Students at all readiness levels have maximum opportunity for challenge, growth, and success.
		Fixed Mindset	**Growth Mindset**
		TEACHER	

Reprinted with permission from Solution Tree.

It is unlikely that a fixed mindset teacher exerts enough effort to ensure the success of a student whom that teacher (consciously or unconsciously) believes is incapable of success. Differentiation is a growth mindset endeavor—it asks teachers to find an academic entry point relative to essential learning outcomes, to make instructional plans designed to move students to mastery of those outcomes from their current points of proficiency, and to adopt a "whatever it takes" approach in doing so. Differentiation also calls on teachers to work with students to show them the direct link between "informed effort" and achievement, thus enlisting each student's energy in their own success.

Dweck (2000, 2017) counsels that we serve our students best not by telling them they are smart but by being candid about where their skills are at a given time and where they need to be in order to achieve their life and school aspirations. She continues, "The confidence students need is not the confidence that they have a certain level of smartness, or that they have more of it than other students. The confidence they need is the confidence that they, or *anybody* for that matter, can learn if they apply their effort and strategies [that support success]" (Dweck, 2000, pp. 57–58).

A belief in the capacity of virtually all students to learn essential content causes teachers to ask questions like these:

- How do I understand the mindset of each of my students in order to ensure that they understand their capacity to impact their own success?
- How do I help each student develop and extend the attitudes, habits of mind, and strategies needed to contribute to their success as a learner?
- How do I understand and address each student's learning development and needs relative to designated learning outcomes for my grade/subject(s)?
- How do I ensure that I position each learner as a thinker and problem solver?
- How do I ensure the supply of materials and support needed for each student's progress?
- How do I ensure that classroom working arrangements build on students' cultural preferences for learning?
- In what ways can I make clear to my students that I value their effort rather than their innate ability—that I am much more interested in their growth than their starting points?
- How do I ensure that competition against oneself, rather than against one another, is the goal of this class?
- How do I ensure that student growth is a key and visible component in reporting grades?

Belief 5: Each student should have equity of access to excellent learning opportunities

A belief in the worth of each student should lead us to conclude that virtually every young person requires access to the best learning opportunities a school has to offer. To suggest that some students require less is to retrench on a deeply important ideal. Here is John Dewey's take:

> What the best and wisest parent wants for his own child, that must the community want for all of its children. Any other ideal for our schools is narrow and unlovely; acted upon, it destroys our democracy.... Only by being true to the full growth of all the individuals who make it up, can society by any chance be true to itself. (in Schlechty, 1997, p. 77)

A belief in the capacity of all students to learn the essential knowledge, understandings, and skills in a topic or unit of study suggests that schools offer their very best to everyone. This belief also implies two additional assumptions. First, learning opportunities should focus on what is essential to learn—that is, on how the subject makes sense and what makes it authentic, useful, relevant, transferable, and meaningful. Second, the curriculum and instruction to which all learners are exposed should provide consistent opportunities to understand the content so students can retain, apply, and transfer what they learn (Tomlinson, 2021, Tomlinson & McTighe, 2006). In other words, if our schools and teachers operated from a growth mindset perspective, we would have little reason to assume that only a few students could learn conceptually, think critically, debate ideas, and address real-world issues. Rather than develop curriculum that mirrors a belief that only a relatively small proportion of students can do complex work, we would plan "high-end" curriculum for advanced students and then scaffold instruction to make certain each student is supported in achieving and, if possible, exceeding those complex goals (Tomlinson, 2021, 2022).

There is ample evidence spanning many years that the practice of providing high-quality curriculum and instruction for some—but not all—students results in an escalating disadvantage for students who are already at a disadvantage in terms of their opportunity to achieve (e.g., Darling-Hammond, 2001; Domina et al., 2016; Gorsky, 2018). In addition, indications are increasingly clear that establishing expectations for a majority of students to become creators (rather than simply consumers) of knowledge is imperative if we expect all our young people to thrive in and contribute to the world they will enter as they leave school (Berger et al., 2014; Fullan et al., 2018). As DuFour and Eaker (1998) put it, "In today's Information Age… educators must operate from the premise that it is the purpose of schools to bring all students to their full potential and to a level of education that was once reserved for the very few" (p. 62).

A belief in equity of access to excellent learning opportunities leads teachers to ask questions like these:

- To what degree does the curriculum feel relevant and engaging to each student in my class?
- Is the curriculum designed to ensure student understanding of content?
- Am I confident that I am "teaching up" to *all* of my students, rather than "watering down" for some of them?

- Are all of the tasks I offer respectful—that is, are they equally appealing and focused on essential understandings, do they require students to think critically and/or creatively, and do they ask all students to work with content in authentic ways?
- In what ways can I make certain that my most advanced students are being consistently challenged?
- In what ways can I support each student in achieving and, whenever possible, surpassing established goals?
- How do I ensure that each student is an active participant in discussions designed to help them make meaning of ideas?
- How do I schedule our time so students can regularly focus on their own specific academic needs and still come together around important ideas?
- How do I consistently seek student input to shape what I ask them to learn?

Belief 6: A central goal of teaching is to maximize the capacity of each learner

Ensuring that each student experiences the best curriculum and instruction a school can offer, as well as the support necessary to succeed in such settings, would move schools much closer to this belief. In practice, however, we generally fall short of embracing it for at least two reasons. First, we tend to accept a single performance level as adequate or even desirable for a grade level. While it is obviously important to have clear learning targets for teachers and students, when we assume that all students reach their maximum respective potential if they achieve the same goals under the same circumstances on the same day, we operate in direct contradiction to all that we know about human development. While, for some students, success is inevitably out of reach on the date designated to judge their competence, other students are invariably rated as "successful" without regard for the fact that they may have passed the performance level measured by the test much earlier in the year.

Students learn incrementally from their various starting points. It is simply how the process works. We cannot require students to make an impossible leap over a chasm in knowledge, nor should we ask them to move backward in order to stay with the class. Theodore Sizer (1985) explains it this way:

One cannot succeed at something totally beyond one's experience, beyond one's grasp. One is interested in that at which one succeeds. Thus, a clever teacher sets a student's work, and the expectations for it, at a level where some modicum of legitimate success is possible. However, because "experience has shown that it is worth the effort to provide the growing child with problems that tempt him into next stages of development," an effective teacher keeps the subject of study at an arm's length from the student, but no further. The joy of success comes especially sweet when that which was mastered had earlier seemed unachievable. (p. 167)

This is the case for students at all entry points into a lesson or unit.

Further, when we set a single benchmark for all students, it is inevitably a middling one. In doing so, we teach students that there is a finish line and that "good enough" is good enough. Former U.S. Secretary of Education John Gardner (1961) reminded us that we are in peril if the goal we set for ourselves is one of amicable mediocrity. All we can ask of students is that they invest maximum effort in learning—and we should not settle for less from our students or from ourselves.

A second reason that our classrooms aren't geared to maximize the capacity of each learner is that we tend to see and think of our students as a group (Brighton et al., 2005; Tomlinson, 2021, 2022). We say, "The *students* always love it when we do this lab," or "The *students* don't understand inverting fractions," or "The *students* were restless today." No doubt a number of students *do* like the lab, *don't* understand how and when to invert fractions, and *were* restless today, but there's also little doubt that some students found the lab pointless or confusing, could *teach* a cogent lesson on inverting fractions, and were perfectly calm and ready to learn today. It's virtually impossible to attend to student differences when we think of "the students" as a single entity. Such thinking also reinforces the sense that a single learning indicator or set of indicators is appropriate for "the students" at a given time. As Baruti Kafele (2021) reminds us,

Each student has their own individuality, academically, socially, and emotionally. And each student has their own voice, academically, socially, and emotionally. Each student is somebody. Each student is somebody special. Each student has his or her own set of experiences, realities, challenges, obstacles, goals, aspirations, and ambitions. Additionally, each student has his or her own unique way of being motivated and inspired. What sets one student on fire might not be what sets another student on fire. Most importantly, how each student learns, thinks, makes sense out of, and processes new information may be unique. (p. 16)

Differentiation asks teachers to look beyond "groupthink" and study the evolving profiles of students as individuals. The degree to which a teacher melds respect for the individual and belief in the capacity of the individual to succeed with the intent to know each student as an individual determines the likelihood that the goal of maximizing the capacity of each learner is operationalized. Such a triumvirate of beliefs also results in many more students exceeding the unitary standard(s) we now establish. Berger (2003) and Berger and colleagues (2014) commend the idea of inspiring each student to create "beautiful work" and ensuring that each learner has the support necessary to achieve "exemplary status" on every summative assessment and every long-term learning target. The work of excellence, Berger (2003) argues, is transformational:

> Once a student sees that he or she is capable of excellence, that student is never quite the same. There is a new self-image, a new notion of possibility. There is an appetite for excellence. After students have had a taste of excellence, they're never quite satisfied with less; they're always hungry. (p. 8)

A belief in the importance of maximizing the capacity of each learner leads teachers to ask questions like these:

- What is *this* student's next step in learning essential content today?
- How can I help each student understand and contribute to their next step in learning?
- What task, materials, and working arrangements will push *this* student a bit beyond their comfort zone today?
- What models and indicators can I use to help *this* student understand what high-quality work looks like at their stage of growth?
- How can I tap into *this* student's motivation to strive for quality?
- What forms of support does *this* student need from me and from peers to persist in the face of difficulty and do exemplary work?
- How do we support one another in working for quality?
- How do we chart growth and quality of work over time?
- How do we recognize and celebrate excellence, both individually and as a community of learners?

A Philosophical Compass for the Journey Ahead

Good teaching—the really good stuff—is hard work. Being a good teacher requires meeting many of the same demands as being a good parent, a good doctor, or a good musician. Humans are largely sustained in our work by a belief that what we do makes a profound difference in the lives of other people. Differentiation is an individual-focused approach to teaching. It is the manifestation of a conviction that *every* student is both unique and of prime importance as a learner and as a human being. It is an affirmation that human differences are normal and desirable, and that excellent teachers plan, teach, and reflect with those differences in mind. Here's how Grant Wiggins (1992) put it:

> We will not successfully restructure schools to be effective until we stop seeing diversity in students as a problem. Our challenge is not one of getting "special" students to better adjust to the usual schoolwork, the usual teacher pace, or the usual tests. The challenge of schooling remains what it has been since the modern era began two centuries ago: ensuring that all students receive their entitlement. They have the *right* to thought-provoking and enabling schoolwork so that they might use their minds well and discover the joy therein to be willing to push themselves farther. They have the *right* to instruction that obligates the teacher, like the doctor, to change tactics when progress fails to occur. They have the *right* to assessment that provides students and teachers with insight into real-world standards…. Until such a time, we will have no insight into human potential. Until the challenge is met, schools will continue to reward the lucky or the already-equipped and weed out the poor performers. (pp. xv–xvi)

Enter the Students

A philosophy in the abstract is worthwhile since it grounds our thinking and reminds us that a life well lived or a career well spent is likely to be more reasoned and purposeful than random. The test of that philosophy comes in the arena of daily life rather than in the seclusion of individual minds. In the case of teaching, a defensible philosophy supports the capacity of teachers to address the needs of the young people in their care.

Abraham Maslow (1943) found that individuals develop along a continuum of needs, with the more basic human needs demanding attention before higher-level needs can be satisfied. First in line, he tells us, are physiological needs for things such as food, clothing, shelter, and sleep. The primacy of these needs is so great that, when there is a deficiency in one or more of them, the body focuses almost exclusively on attending to that need. In a school setting, students who enter the classroom hungry, cold, sleepy, or worried about where they will find shelter at night have no mental energy to learn a new language or complete a worksheet—until a teacher or another adult can attend to their needs.

Once physiological needs are met, the need for safety and security takes center stage. For these needs to be satisfied, students require a sense that they are not only physically safe but also safe from teasing, bullying, and hopelessness in terms of the tasks and challenges ahead. A school and classroom that provide safety and model and demand respect can help pave the way to effective learning, but when the end of the day nears and the student again faces potential threats, anticipation of the dangers ahead will push learning aside. Only when safety and security seem assured can individuals systematically seek acknowledgment and belonging. Most students want to be part of a community. A feeling of collegiality or "teamwork" in the classroom satisfies this need to be a part of (rather than apart from) the group. The absence of such a sense of belonging leads to loneliness, isolation, and low self-esteem. In school, it essentially derails the learning process.

When an individual's physiological needs are adequately addressed, attention can then be spent on esteem needs such as academic learning. When this is the case, students demonstrate a desire to engage themselves in ways that bring recognition and value. They want to contribute and be valued as contributors to the group and its work. Through achievement, they develop a sense of self-efficacy.

The final two levels of Maslow's hierarchy of needs are self-actualization, in which an individual strives to become all that they can be, and self-transcendence, in which individuals learn to live at a higher level of insight and on a plane that takes them beyond themselves. It is highly unusual for young people to achieve these two stages.

It is interesting, then, to realize that academic learning requires students to work at the highest level of need satisfaction within their grasp as young people. It certainly reminds us, once again, that a teacher's job is not simply to enter a room and impart knowledge, but rather to attend to each student as a whole human being in order to open the way for each student to truly become a learner.

When we keep Maslow's hierarchy in mind, we realize that most learners come to school not so much to seek mastery of math or literature as to satisfy more basic needs, such as affirmation and contribution. Once those needs have been met, they shift their attention to things such as purpose, challenge, and power (Tomlinson, 2004, 2021, 2022). A teacher who honors the individual seeks to understand each student's particular progression of needs and to address those needs in a way that leads to both personal and academic growth.

The Teacher Responds

Students *will* come to school with the sorts of needs—both cognitive and affective—outlined by Maslow. Teachers *will* respond to those needs—by addressing them or ignoring them, understanding the similarities and differences in how students experience them or generalizing across students. At least two elements determine a teacher's response to students' needs and its quality in terms of student benefits. One determinant is the philosophy (or lack thereof) that shapes the teacher's actions. The second determinant is the teacher's level of competency in setting and following a specific course of action. We often think of these two elements as "will" and "skill." Ultimately, a philosophy of teaching is based first on a teacher's will to teach each learner and then on that teacher's will to develop the skills required to understand every learner and teach them as individuals.

We hope this chapter will contribute to the development of beliefs about the nature and purpose of teaching. We also hope that the following chapters will contribute to teachers' skills in managing and leading a classroom that is attentive to learners' particular needs and to the group's common needs. A philosophy of teaching based on beliefs such as the ones outlined earlier in this chapter leads teachers to respond to student needs for affirmation, purpose, challenge, and power with invitation, investment, persistence, opportunity, and reflection (Tomlinson, 2004, 2021, 2022). In a variety of ways and over time, teachers need to consistently convey the following messages to their students, both individually and as a whole class:

- **Invitation**—I am pleased that you are here, eager to know you better, and aware that you bring important experiences and characteristics to class with you. I see you with unconditional positive regard—that is, the belief that you are valuable and worthy of respect as you are. I want to do whatever I can to make this a place of learning for you. I encourage you to help me be the best teacher possible for you.
- **Investment**—Because you are important in this class and in the world, I am going to work hard to help you grow as much and as fast as you can. Because your effort has much to do with your success, I am going to ask you to work hard as well. I will help you develop the attitudes and skills that support the hard work of learning.

- **Persistence**—You won't always get things right the first time you try them. Neither will I. When class is not going well for you, I am going to work for you and with you to find approaches that will ensure your success. I will never give up on you.

- **Opportunity**—You are young and just learning about the possibilities that exist in the world. I want to provide opportunities for you to see yourself at work in varied settings, in varied roles, and with varied content. This is a time for you to prepare for the future and get excited by the possibilities that exist for you.

- **Reflection**—I will listen to you, learn from you, observe you at work in our class, study your progress, and ask for your guidance. I will think about my work and how it's working for you as often as I possibly can. I expect that of myself so that I can become a more aware and effective teacher. I will ask the same of you so you can become a more aware and effective learner.

In addition to this sort of affective response to a student's needs, a teacher whose work is rooted in the worth of the individual understands that much of what they communicate to students will be in the form of curriculum and instruction. Therefore, the teacher ensures that every student's work is engaging, important, focused, challenging, and scaffolded (Tomlinson, 2004, 2021). These attributes of day-to-day work clearly communicate to students the teacher's belief in their individual worth and potential.

In a book that is both disturbing and hopeful, Kirsten Olson (2009) presents her body of research, which includes interviews with many adults from diverse backgrounds, virtually all of whom felt profoundly "wounded by school." Olson didn't set out to do research in this area; the work evolved as she discovered that many adults with whom she spoke (about other topics) discussed negative impacts that school had on them. She goes on to clarify that her definition of "wounded by school" does not include the inevitable moments of discomfort that occur when substantial numbers of young people share a classroom or the kinds of natural "bumps and bruises" that help us grow. Instead, she's talking about the hurt that diminishes individuals in their own eyes, doesn't go away even in adulthood, and cannot be dismissed even if the victim achieves success in the eyes of the world. Common results of such wounding that emerged from the interviews included the following:

• A loss of pleasure in learning.

• A belief that we are not smart or competent in learning.

• A belief that our abilities are fixed and can't be improved with effort, coaching, or self-understanding.

• A belief that we are "just average" in a way that feels diminishing.

• Anger toward teachers and others in authority because we feel that we are not seen or acknowledged as worthy.

• A generalized feeling of shame that came from school and produces generalized anxiety.

• A sense that school diminished us cognitively.

• A low appetite for intellectual risk taking; in other words, a desire to get the right answer and just finish the job.

Olson finds that there are some teachers who heal wounds, and as a group, they exhibit predictable behaviors. These teachers

• Welcome and honor diversity in race, language, economic status, learning exceptionality, gender, and sexual orientation.

• Accept many types of students and consciously value diversity of background and experience in the classroom.

• Place the student at the center of instruction.

• Honor what students already know and feel.

• Honor varied ways in which students most comfortably learn.

• Emphasize multiple avenues of content presentation, reflection, and assessment.

• Make communities of caring central to learning.

• Acknowledge the ambiguity inherent in teaching.

• Employ experimentation in instructional design and learn from mistakes.

It is not a great leap to suggest that a philosophy of differentiation exists to avoid wounding learners (as much as those wounds are within our power to avoid) and to play a role in healing the wounds that young learners bring with them into the classroom. Philosophically, differentiation is an approach that commends planning for human wholeness as a primary goal—and that provides for healing when necessary. Accepting this premise provides teachers with considerable guidance when they plan for instruction, reflect on instruction, and talk with others about the work they do.

Nora Rose, a graduate student at the University of Virginia, reflected, "I have come to see differentiation not as something revolutionary but as a kind of quiet radicalism. This is not meant to discount its power but rather to highlight it as a practice of kindness." Nora's statement reflects a core insight about differentiation. A teacher who works from deep and determined respect for the worth of each learner will, through study and practice, discover differentiation—not all at once, but step by step—as part of the search for ways to dignify and extend the capacities of each of those learners.

Chapter 3 explores ways in which teachers invite students to share in the development of a philosophy of differentiation. It also examines how teachers assume the role as leader of parents, colleagues, and administrators in understanding and supporting differentiation.

3

The Invitation to the Vision
Talking with Students, Parents, and Other Educators About Differentiation

> Treating students as people comes very close to "living" the academic, personal, and social educational goals that are stated in most official policy documents. But more than that, involving students in constructing their own meaning and learning is fundamentally pedagogically essential—they learn more and are motivated to go even further.
>
> —Michael Fullan, *The New Meaning of Educational Change,* 3rd Edition

A frequent comment from teachers who are early in their consideration of differentiation is "My students would be angry if they saw that someone else had a different book or a different activity than they did in a lesson." Interestingly, that is an issue almost never raised by teachers who are practitioners of differentiation. So why the difference?

Chances are good that the first teacher is operating from the common belief system about teaching and learning—and that their students are as well. Among the tenets of that belief system is a common curriculum for everyone and, thus, a "right" or "standard" lesson that all students in the class must complete to ensure orderly coverage of the content. In that paradigm, a good teacher makes sure everyone does the same thing in a given lesson and uses a standard set of materials, standard pacing, and a standard support system. Not only is that the correct way to "do school," but it's also the "fair" way. Therefore, a teacher who does something different for one or a few students is at risk of being seen as unfair.

The second teacher is operating from a different belief system. This teacher believes that there is a common set of critical content that every student should learn and that their job as a teacher is to ensure that each student has the best possible opportunity to master and, if possible, move beyond that content. In this paradigm, the teacher understands that students enter each segment of learning at varied starting points, bring different experiences to which they can connect new learning, work at different speeds, process information in a variety of ways, and require different support systems in order to master the essential content. Thus, while this teacher is committed to ensuring that each student succeeds with designated learning outcomes, the teacher also recognizes the need to provide a range of ways for students to access information, a variety of options for processing or making sense of the information, an array of support systems, and multiple outlets for students to demonstrate what they learn. In this teacher's way of thinking, treating all students exactly alike is counterproductive. It's necessary to meet students where they are in terms of readiness, interest, and approaches to learning in order to maximize their academic growth.

The first teacher envisions using a differentiated instructional strategy in an environment that values sameness—one in which treating everyone alike is the gold standard. It feels as though it would be changing the rules of a game without telling the players, and some level of anarchy is likely to result. The second teacher is aware that most students come to class with a standard set of rules firmly ingrained in their thinking (unless a prior teacher differentiated instruction or there is schoolwide attention to differentiation). This teacher has no intention of trying to "sneak" differentiation into daily routines. There's no thought of "doing" differentiation *to* students; it's about doing differentiation *with* them. Therefore, from the first day of school, the second teacher sees students as partners in success. From the first day of school, this teacher works consistently to build a shared classroom vision and to construct with students the processes and procedures that support the success of that vision. In other words, this teacher will serve as a leader in establishing an effectively differentiated classroom.

This chapter discusses specific goals for teachers who want to lead students and develop classrooms designed to support student success with critical content, specific ways in which teachers might engage their students in understanding and contributing to a differentiated classroom, and various conversations that enable teachers and students to develop a common sense of direction in the classroom. It also briefly discusses the teacher as a leader in helping both parents and other educators understand and contribute to differentiation.

A Framework for Coming Together

At the beginning of the year, a teacher who wants to lead students to understand and contribute to a differentiated classroom will invest some start-up time in the process. There may be a few class periods or time slots that focus largely on conversations and activities related to differentiation, and there will be a number of others in which more abbreviated conversations or decision-making sessions occur.

The idea of diverting time from covering curriculum may be distressing to some teachers. Research and teacher experience, however, clearly indicate that students and teachers gain more time than they've lost when they develop a shared vision for their work and a common set of routines that function smoothly for the rest of the year (e.g., Lynch, 2015; Marzano et al., 2003; Stronge, 2018).

Each teacher will need to decide how much time to invest in the topics suggested below and to the start-up and follow-up conversations. With students of any age, it is important to introduce ideas and routines and to review initial conversations briefly throughout the year, helping them refresh their memories about established goals and procedures, reflect on the efficacy of the goals and procedures, and refine those goals and procedures, as necessary.

Regardless of grade level, there are at least six key questions that teachers need to explore with students to help develop a shared understanding of and investment in a differentiated classroom. The wording of these questions may vary according to grade, but the substance remains the same.

1. Who are you as learners? (*Are you all alike or are there important differences?*)

2. Given the differences we see, how should I teach you? (*How should we learn together?*)

3. If our classroom is going to work for all of us, what will it be like? (*What will it look like? How will it need to function? What roles will each of us play?*)

4. How can I learn more about your starting points, interests, and best ways of learning?

5. If we have a differentiated classroom, can it be fair? (*What will "fair" mean in this room?*)

6. What will success in this class mean? (*How will I know if you're succeeding? How will you know? Will success always mean the same thing for each learner?*)

Pursuit of these questions is evolutionary. In other words, each new question develops from discussions of the previous questions. For example, the fifth question about fairness only really makes sense after the first four questions are discussed. Pursuit of these questions is also recursive; teachers will need to remind students of earlier discussions with a sort of "if/then" logic as the discussions unfold. For example, "If we agree on this idea, then what will we need to do to make it work?" Finally, teachers need to revisit these questions with students at key points during the year to refresh student thinking, provide specific opportunities for students to share successes and concerns, and enable the group to contribute to a maturing of the ideas as the year progresses.

The following sections mirror the logic of these questions to help readers think about what they want their students to consider and how they might go about shaping discussions and activities to engage their students with those ideas.

Who are you as learners?

Arguably, the most important thing that any teacher of any age group in any kind of classroom does at the beginning of each year is convey, through words, actions, and tone, a message of pleasure and excitement at the prospect of getting to know their students. The message has to be an honest one, of course, and when it is, it begins the long journey of building trust between teacher and learners. The message requires consistent and persistent follow-through. It needs to ring true in everything the teacher does. If trust is established between teacher and students, the latter begin to see themselves as acceptable and even valuable. They see the teacher as worthy of their trust, class content becomes more important, and learning becomes worth the risk it inevitably involves.

In a differentiated classroom, the teacher takes the message further. The message is not simply "I want to know you as people." It becomes "Knowing you individually will necessarily shape how I teach you." The implication is clear: "How could I really care to know what your strengths, needs, and interests are without wanting to act upon that knowledge in order to teach you well?"

The goals of the first conversation are to help students (1) recognize that the teacher cares about them as people and wants to know them, (2) begin to share a bit about themselves, (3) consider the similarities and differences among class-mates, and (4) think about what it would mean to have a classroom designed to work for all kinds of learners. We'll present three suggestions for developing these goals with students, and we invite you to borrow one of these approaches or use them as a foundation to develop your own.

Graphing Me. Having students graph their strengths and weaknesses is an approach that is useful across many grade levels. The format can vary with the age of the students, but the goal is to have students indicate aspects of content about which they feel confident and areas in which they are less sure. Younger students might color in a premade bar graph to indicate their relative strengths and weak-nesses in a variety of subject areas such as reading, art, math, writing, science, and so on. It can be useful to ask students to respond to some areas that are not directly related to school (e.g., being a friend, doing chores on time, making up games). Figure 3.1 (see p. 68) shows a graph completed by a 2nd grade student along with the student's comments on her self-assessment.

Older students might follow directions to create a bar or line graph with relevant skills along the horizontal axis (e.g., computation, problem solving, frac-tions, equations, mathematical writing). It can be helpful to ask students to add two or three topics to the horizontal axis that do not directly relate to course con-tent (such as hobbies or nonacademic skills) or that relate to a different course (such as math and sports skills on an English language arts graph). On the vertical axis, students should place descriptors that indicate a range of performance from poor to outstanding. (It's fun for the class and teacher to create the descriptors together so that the words reflect the language of the learners.)

To introduce this activity, it's a good idea for the teacher to complete a graph as students observe. This allows the teacher to model the assignment in a thoughtful way, enables the teacher to introduce some ideas that may be impor-tant as the year goes on, and helps students to get to know the teacher better. For example, the teacher may have some areas of relative weakness, areas in which they have not achieved their potential, or an area in which they were once weak and perhaps even afraid but are now competent. As part of this process, we recommend that teachers create overlapping or dual graphs that illustrate growth from "then" (when the teacher was a student) to "now."

Figure 3.1

Mika's Strengths and Weaknesses Bar Graph

	Reading	Writing	Math	Drawing	Ballet
Excellent					
Great					
Good					
Fair					
Poor					

"*I am excellent at reading. I am good at writing. I am great at math and drawing. I am excellent at ballet because I've been in ballet for five years. I am worse at drawing than ballet. I am worse at writing than reading. I am better at math than writing. I am worse at writing than math. I am better at ballet than math and drawing. I am excellent at reading even though I have not done it as long as ballet.*"

Figure 3.2 provides an example of a graph completed by a 7th grade language arts teacher for her class. The dark bars represent her proficiency when she was a young student, and the lighter bars indicate her current profile in the same area. As she creates her graph, she tells her students that she was an excellent speller when she was in elementary school, but she is now a weaker speller because she has read so many papers written by 7th graders who spell words in so many different ways, apparently causing her to absorb some of their spellings. Likewise, she was a strong math student in elementary school, but she lost both skills and confidence when she began to fall behind in an 8th grade algebra class and the teacher never noticed. Her experience in that one class negatively impacted her math performance for the rest of her school years. By contrast, she explains to her students that she had always loved words and playing with words, and her pleasure and success in that area led to her becoming an English teacher.

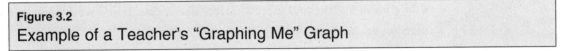

Figure 3.2
Example of a Teacher's "Graphing Me" Graph

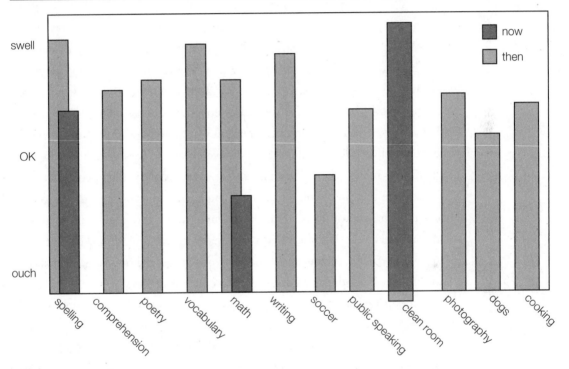

When students complete their graphs, they should share one or two items with either the whole class (which provides a great opportunity for the teacher to observe and make notes on each student's presenting skills, speech patterns, and interests) or with a small group of peers. They can then post their graphs around the classroom, and younger students can walk around the room and look for a graph that is just like their own. It is likely that they won't find a graph that is very similar to their own, and they will almost certainly not find an exact duplicate. This realization readies the class for the next step in the discussion. After making a gallery walk to look at all the graphs, older students should complete the following phrase (accurately) in as many ways as possible: *In general, it's true that* _____. They will likely think of many different ways to complete the phrase. For example:

- *In general, it's true that* students in second period say they are better at interpreting lab results than students in third period say they are.
- *In general, it's true that* more boys than girls say they are good at basketball.
- *In general, it's true that* more students like speaking in a world language than like reading in one.

There are two observations that several students in every class nearly always make, and these are particularly important to the continuing discussion: (1) nobody thought they performed the same in everything, and (2) everybody said they have stronger points and weaker points. Whenever one of these conclusions is voiced, it's time for the next step in the discussion. If no one shares either of these two conclusions, the teacher can directly prompt students with a question such as "Did anyone notice that everyone said they were better in some things and worse in others?" With these observations out in the open, the teacher can continue the discussion by saying, "You know, I think about that a lot as a teacher. All of you will be better in some things and less confident in others. It's that way every year. If some of you are great with computation skills but really shaky with problem solving, and others of you are just the opposite, what should I do? How do I decide which one of you to concentrate on?"

Students typically understand the ideas behind differentiation more rapidly than teachers do. They never respond with "It doesn't matter. Don't pay attention to what we can and can't do. Just cover the material." It is likely that they will readily conclude that you should help them develop their various strengths and shore up their areas of weakness. Arriving at this sort of conclusion is the goal of this activity and its associated discussion.

There are, of course, many other ways to engage students and help them think about ways in which they differ as learners. In both of the following activities, the ultimate goal is the same as with this "Graphing Me" exercise: to draw the conclusion that student differences matter and the class will be a better one for them if the teacher teaches with those differences in mind. Regardless of which route the teacher selects to help students consider why their differences as learners are important, this is a good time to make a point that should become a classroom refrain for the remainder of the year:

I teach because I believe every student can be successful in learning what matters most. When you learn, you are stronger people. Every one of you has the potential to learn something new each and every day. The path you follow may or may not be the same as the one followed by the person sitting next to you. That's not important. What is important is that you take your own next step and continue to follow your own path. My job is to work with you and make sure you continue to learn and move along that path. What I want us to figure out together during the next few days—and throughout the year—is how we can work together to create a classroom that supports every single person on their individual paths as well as become stronger as a whole class.

This is the central premise of differentiation, and it's important for students to begin to understand this core assumption.

A Trip to the Doctor. In this role-play, students work with partners. In each pair, one student will play the part of a parent and the other will play the role of the parent's child (who is the same age as your students). The teacher will play the role of a physician. Directions on the cards should specify a particular medical problem that the child is experiencing such as an itchy rash, a stomachache, an arm that was injured in a basketball game, or a headache that comes and goes. Each "child" should act in a way that's appropriate for the malady (e.g., scratching a rash, holding their stomach, cradling their arm, rubbing their forehead) while the "parent" describes the problem to the "physician." For the last two pairs, the role-play cards should indicate that the parent introduces the problem to the doctor and then says, "My child will tell you about it." The students playing the sick children then speak for themselves. Figure 3.3 (see p. 72) shows examples of two role-play cards.

In all cases (regardless of the actual illness), the physician should listen attentively and then say, "I'm so sorry you're not feeling well. Here's some cold medicine. Take it and see if it helps." The last pair of students to participate should role-play a common cold, with the "child" explaining the symptoms experienced in some detail.

By the time the last pair gets to the doctor, the students are generally relieved to find that someone actually has symptoms that match the remedy. The teacher might want to ask, "How many times would you or your parents visit that doctor before you or they decided they weren't very good and you didn't want to go back?"

At some point, it's also good to ask, "Why do you think the adults always talked for their children? At the end, when the students finally spoke up for themselves rather than relying on their parents to speak for them, did they explain the problem well enough for you to get what was wrong?" This sidebar can help introduce the idea that students often know what they need as well as, or better than, adults do and that they should freely say whenever they see a way to make the class better for them.

Figure 3.3
Sample Role-Play Cards

ROLE-PLAY INSTRUCTIONS	ROLE-PLAY INSTRUCTIONS
Scenario:	*Scenario:*
You will play the role of a parent or guardian. Your partner will play the role of your child. The teacher will play the role of a physician.	Your partner will play the role of your parent or guardian. You will play the role of their child. The teacher will play the role of a physician.
Your child is not feeling well because of an itchy and painful rash, so you're at the doctor's office to see if you can get some help for the rash.	You are not feeling well because of a possible broken arm, so you're at the doctor's office to see if you can get some help.
Here's what you should do:	*Here's what you should do:*
Greet the doctor and explain that your child has a really bad rash on their arms. Tell the doctor that it started over the weekend, after you returned from your parents' house. Explain that you think the rash may be poison ivy because your child and their grandfather worked outside a lot, but mention that you're not sure because your child is often in the outdoors and has never had poison ivy. Ask for a prescription to help with the itching and pain.	Act like you feel really uncomfortable. Hold your arm like you're trying to protect it.
Here's what your partner will do:	*Here's what your partner will do:*
They will act like they are very uncomfortable and scratch their arms every once in a while. After the doctor says to not scratch the rash, they will just hold or rub their arms a little.	They will greet the doctor and explain that you hurt your arm in a basketball game last night. They thought it was just a sprain, but the pain got worse all night long and now you can't move your arm. They are worried that your arm might be broken and needs the doctor's help.
Here's what both of you should do:	*Here's what both of you should do:*
When the doctor gives the diagnosis and prescription, react appropriately and leave the doctor's office (go back to your seats).	When the doctor gives the diagnosis and prescription, react appropriately and leave the doctor's office (go back to your seats).

All that's necessary for students to get the point of this role-play is for the teacher to ask, "Why did we just do that? What's it got to do with school?" Students usually respond that it's no more effective in school for a teacher to do the same thing with everyone, no matter their need, than for the doctor to prescribe the same thing to every patient, no matter the symptom. This, again, positions the teacher to say, "I think teachers are like doctors because they should listen to their students, understand their various needs, and work with each student to figure out what is necessary to help that particular student function well. Do you agree?"

One Size Fits All? A third activity that helps students begin to think about classrooms that attend to students' varying needs starts with the teacher asking two students to put on jackets that are clearly the wrong size for them. The teacher selects two students who are very different in height and stature, making sure both of them are comfortable in front of the class (or being the center of attention). The smaller student should put on a jacket that is several sizes too large. After students have had a few moments to giggle, the larger student should attempt to put on a jacket that is several sizes too small.

The two students then describe how they feel in the clothes. Answers are often lighthearted and a little silly. The teacher should allow for a slight pause to consider the answers before asking the two students to describe how they think they'd feel at the end of the day if they had to wear the jackets all day long. Students typically begin to see potential problems that are a little more serious (e.g., "I'd have trouble eating lunch because the sleeves would get in my food" or "I don't think I could write very well because it's hard to move my arms"). Finally, the teacher should ask them to describe what they think would happen if they had to wear clothes of this size all year. Generally, students easily see that what initially seemed silly, unimportant, or slightly inconvenient could become a serious impediment to doing what they like to do (e.g., "I think I'd begin to see myself as a slob" or "I don't know if kids would want me to work with them in school because I couldn't do much to help with projects since I can hardly move").

Once again, it's generally only necessary to ask the class, "Why do you think we just did this? What's it got to do with school or with this class?" Students will often talk about how uncomfortable it is when class activities or assignments are the "wrong size" and it becomes difficult to do the work. They sometimes share examples from their own school experiences when work seemed to always be "too big" or "too small" for them, and they are generally quite able to explain both short-term and long-term fallout from those experiences.

As is the case with the previous two examples, this activity easily leads to the conclusion "When you look around the room, it's clear that not everyone wears the same size clothes. My experience as a teacher has shown me just as clearly that identical assignments won't always be a good fit for everyone in the classroom either. What do you think a teacher should do about the fact that not all students are exactly alike in their needs at a particular time?" With this question in mind, students should be ready to move to the next step in the discussion.

Given the differences we see, how should I teach you?

Whether the teacher elects to use one of the three activities explained above or develop another approach, it is important for students to consider the reality that people don't come in matched sets like luggage. Human differences are not only normal—they are valuable. If we were all clones of one another, the world would be much less interesting and people would be much less prepared to address the issues and problems that are inevitable in life. We'd exhibit very limited creativity.

In this portion of the conversation, the teacher should pose some grade-level or subject-specific questions for students to consider. Here are some examples:

- Let's say there are some students in our physics class who are very strong in science but haven't had chemistry yet. Would you expect any important learner needs to arise that are specific to this group of students? What should I do about them?
- What if we have some students in our class who have no trouble memorizing spelling words and we have some other students who always find spelling to be the hardest thing they do? Does it make sense that both groups of students should always have exactly the same spelling words? Would they all learn equally well if they always had the same words?
- What if we have some students in our class who are often happiest and most productive when they work in groups and we have others who generally prefer to learn alone? Whose preference should I honor when I'm trying to decide how to set up the class for work we need to accomplish?
- Suppose we have some students in our Spanish class who have a great ear for language. They can repeat almost everything they hear me say, and they do it accurately. On the other hand, writing in Spanish is a chore for them. No matter how hard they work, they can't seem to write as quickly, or as accurately, as some other students. Likewise, suppose we have some students who write in Spanish easily, but they get knots in their stomach when they have to speak in class. Does any of that matter? Is there a way I could be a better teacher for all students? Is there a way that we could set up the class to work better for everyone's unique needs?

As the class discusses particular scenarios, students should work together to name specific ways in which they could be more flexible so more of their classmates get what they need to succeed. Here are some examples:

- It might be better if students could choose books to read that interested them rather than always having to read the same assigned books.
- Some students might already know a lot about what we're getting ready to study, and it would be better for them to do work that is new and challenging for them.
- It might be better if we had a choice of ways to show what we are learning. Some students might want to write about it, but others might do a better job of making a chart or doing a video demonstration.
- It might help if we could work with friends to learn something or get help when we don't understand something. Some students might do better trying to figure out an idea alone, or they could work with the teacher to get unstuck.
- Some of us might need longer to work on something in order to get it done right.
- Some of us might want to work longer on something because we like it a lot and want to learn more about it.
- Some of us might learn better if the teacher used demonstrations and examples instead of only lecturing.
- Some of us might learn better if we get to try out an idea instead of just hearing about it.

The point of this segment of the shared conversation is for students to begin to imagine and articulate some ways in which they might learn better if the classroom provided more options. It's good for as many ideas as possible to come from the students, but it's also effective for the teacher to offer some ideas for consideration. Pause every so often to ask questions such as "How do these ideas sound to you? What sounds positive about them, and what are some concerns you have?" It's not necessary to address particular concerns at this point, but it might be wise to list them for future discussions as the conversation moves ahead.

If our classroom is going to work for all of us, what will it be like?

At this stage, students need to begin to work with the teacher to move from an idea to a practical reality. In other words, it's now important to talk about

(1) what the classroom might look like and (2) what role each person will need to play, as well as what they shouldn't do, in order to contribute to the success of everyone in the classroom. Again, appropriate language and length of time spent on any segment of the conversation will vary with students' ages, the teacher's goals for the conversation, and the context of the class. In all cases, however, the goal is to set early expectations for classroom operation and establish shared responsibility for its success.

A number of these elements will be discussed in greater detail in Part II of this book. Here, however, we'll propose some of the big ideas or principles that make a flexible classroom work. The goal is to help students think about what will help everyone learn as much and as efficiently as possible. This includes, but is not limited to, opportunities for each student to

- Use materials that are a good fit for their personal learning needs and interests.
- Connect important ideas to personal experiences and interests.
- Work with knowledge and skills that are at their next step in growth.
- Work at a pace that supports learning.
- Receive help from the teacher and peers that supports their growth and success.
- Explore ideas and skills in ways that are effective and efficient.
- Express learning in ways that best show what they have learned.
- Learn with and from a variety of classmates.
- Teach a variety of classmates.
- Learn how to be a more independent learner, to develop agency as a learner.
- Learn how to be a better group member and partner.

A classroom in which these opportunities are available (when appropriate) suggests a setting with the following characteristics:

- Students sometimes work alone and sometimes work in small groups of peers.
- Working groups are sometimes homogeneous and sometimes heterogeneous, based sometimes on student readiness, sometimes on student interests, sometimes on approach, and may be formed around student choice, formed around teacher choice, or random.

- Students work sometimes with the teacher as a whole class and sometimes individually or in small groups.
- Students have access to many kinds of materials that support learning, including multiple sets of reading materials, digital resources, and video and audio resources.
- Room arrangements are flexible—furniture and working spaces can be rearranged depending on need.
- Students are sometimes able to finish their work at different times.
- Students sometimes have different in-class assignments.
- Students sometimes have different homework assignments.
- The teacher sometimes works with individuals or small groups while the rest of the class works independently or in small groups.

If there are particular elements that the teacher feels should be implemented early in the school year, those elements should be part of the discussion. If students raise possibilities that seem to suggest more than the teacher feels is manageable early in the year, then it's a good idea to keep a running list (perhaps on chart paper so students can see their ideas recorded and return to them when needed); that list will grow throughout the year as students continue to think of and add new ideas and routines. Expect to fine-tune ideas as everyone begins to work with them.

Once students and the teacher have proposed a fundamental set of ideas or procedures that are essential to a differentiated, flexible, or responsive classroom, it's time to consider the implications of those elements for everyone involved. The teacher might begin this consideration by saying, "Let's take a closer look at a few of the ideas we have raised and talk about what each person in the class will need to do, or avoid doing, so the ideas can work well for everyone. This should help us get started smoothly as we begin our work this year."

In the beginning, present the elements that are critical to implementing differentiation and fundamental to operating a flexible classroom. Raise the points with which you will need the greatest amount of student understanding and cooperation. Figure 3.4 (see p. 78) suggests some of these elements and some of the implications for both the teacher and students.

While the particulars will vary among classrooms, the discussion this activity sparks should help students begin to understand *why* they will be asked to make certain choices, do certain things, not do others, and work in specific ways. More students will work more effectively from a shared rationale or vision than from a static set of abstract rules posted on the wall.

Figure 3.4

Critical Elements in a Differentiated Classroom and Their Implications

Goal/Element in a Flexible Classroom	Implications for the Teacher	Implications for Students
Students need to	*The teacher*	*Students*
Work in small groups with classmates.	• Will ensure that all groups have assignments that work for the group so everyone learns what they need to learn. • Will ensure that each group has clear directions. • Will ensure that students know how to work together effectively. • Will provide directions for moving furniture to allow for a variety of groupings.	• Will focus on what their group should do rather than focusing on what others are doing. • Will ensure that they understand the directions given to their group and will follow them. • Will contribute to the effectiveness of their group and ask for help when there is a problem the group can't solve. • Will monitor their conversations so noise doesn't detract from learning. • Will move furniture smoothly so groups have appropriate spaces to work.
Work individually with the teacher or in small groups.	• Will know what each student requires in order to learn at a given time so the groups support learning. • Will ensure that student directions are clear and that students have ways to get help when the teacher is busy with a small group or individual. • Will keep track of student needs, work, and growth and help students do the same for themselves.	• Will be able to start and stop individual and small-group work efficiently to meet with the teacher when necessary. • Will not interrupt when the teacher is working with individuals or groups. • Will know how to get help when the teacher is busy with groups or individuals. • Will keep track of their own learning goals and work toward those goals.
Spend different amounts of time on a task in order to learn well.	• Will provide a place for students to turn in completed work and get it checked if necessary. • Will provide options for important student work when a task is finished (i.e., anchor activities).	• Will follow directions about turning in work or getting it checked when it's finished. • Will work with anchor activities smoothly and effectively when an assignment is completed to show the student's best work.
Work with different materials in order to learn well.	• Will provide a variety of materials that work for students' different entry points, including language needs, interests, and formats. • Will help develop a way to make sure students know which materials to use at a particular time and where materials will be stored.	• Will help make sure materials are cared for and returned to the place they belong after an activity is completed. • Will help the teacher know which materials (or kinds of materials) work best for them as individuals.

How can I learn more about your starting points, interests, and best ways of learning?

Clearly, differentiation is based on acceptance of the reality that learning is shaped by a variety of factors, including prior experiences, culture, economics, language, interests, learning preferences, and support systems. To teach a student well, a teacher must know that student well. That is a formidable charge, and the truth is that no teacher will ever know any of their students fully. However, this should not suggest that it is impossible for a teacher to learn systematically about students at a level that supports differentiated, personalized, or responsive teaching.

Over time, a teacher should aspire to know some general things, such as how well the students read, what they like to do with their spare time, what their dreams are, how they relate to their peers, how they see themselves as learners, what helps them learn best, and how their culture shapes them as learners. As various aspects of the curriculum unfold, the teacher needs to know whether students bring with them prerequisite knowledge and skills, what they understand and misunderstand, the degree to which they have mastered or surpassed expectations at a given time, which instructional approaches work well for them and which do not, and whether they can connect key ideas to their personal lives and experiences. When students come to class with varied stresses, anxieties, and challenges that consume much of their energy, it's important for the teacher to work consistently to understand those challenges. This is the best way to ensure both the teacher and student peers can provide effective support for members of the class who carry heavy weights, rather than contributing to those weights.

In an effectively differentiated classroom, ongoing assessment informs every important instructional decision a teacher makes. Early in the year, students need to know that their teacher is also a student who diligently studies two things: the content that's the focus of instruction and the students themselves. This message needs to be clear from the first day of school and evident every day that follows. At some point in the early conversations about creating a classroom that supports each student's success, it is important for students to hear the following:

- I want to know you as a person because you're interesting to me.
- I need to know you as a student so that I can understand what sorts of learning experiences will be relevant and challenging for you. I will watch you as you work in class as closely as I can because what I learn will help me plan better for you individually and for the class as a whole.

• You'll see me take notes while you work and while we discuss things in class. This helps me learn more about how learning works for you.

• During the first few days of school, I'll ask you to do some things that will give me a reasonable sense of your starting points this year and about who you are as a learner.

• Throughout the year, I'll often ask you to share what you're learning so that I can help you take your next step as a learner.

• Much of the time, I'll be less interested in grading your work and more interested in giving you feedback that will help you learn more robustly and increase your chances of success when I *do* grade your work.

• I'll often invite you to tell me how you're feeling about your work and what is going well or poorly for you in class. I hope you'll always feel free to honestly tell me those things, even if I forget to ask.

Depending on the students' age and the nature of the class, they might be prompted to express what they wish their teachers knew about them, how they think teachers could use what they learn about students in order to teach better, or how teachers might get to know them better and faster. Remember that the goal here is to clarify for students that they have a role to play in articulating how their teacher will continually learn about them in order to be more effective for each of them. It also lets students know that an assessment of their strengths, needs, and interests will begin almost immediately. Students, too, need to begin to understand that teaching and learning work better when everyone knows what the learning targets are, when the teacher and a particular student know where that student is in relation to the target at a given time, and when both use that information to move ahead.

If we have a differentiated classroom, can it be fair?

While the four questions posed prior to this one should generally be pursued with students during the first few days of school, the question of "fairness" is probably best introduced after the class has begun to work in a differentiated setting and after routines to support differentiation are largely in place. In other words, the first significant conversation about fairness should take place after students have enough experience in a differentiated classroom to understand its rationale and to have experienced how it works for them as individuals and as a group. Depending on the particular setting, that might mean at the end of the first month of school or perhaps a little later or a little earlier.

The teacher might begin the conversation by reviewing some of the goals, procedures, and routines the group previously discussed that are now in place. Then the teacher might say something like, "It's been useful to me to hear your ideas about these things as we've begun to create our classroom. I have an additional question I'd like to get your thinking on today. It's often the case that people say a classroom is fair when everyone does everything alike—or when a teacher makes sure everyone gets exactly the same work and materials and time allotments for work. As we've agreed, however, it's not always the most effective approach for everyone to do everything alike. Does that make our classroom unfair? What do you think 'fair' means in this classroom?"

Student responses will vary for a range of reasons. Often, however, early in the year, students in differentiated classroom will suggest that the class is fair if the teacher seems to like everyone alike or doesn't seem to have favorites. Sometimes, students will say the class is fair if the teacher pays attention to everyone.

Over time, if a differentiated classroom is working as it should, students will generally conclude that the class is fair if everyone gets what they need in order to succeed. The shift from "fair = identical treatment" to "fair = equity of opportunity to grow and succeed" is an important one because it embodies the nature and intent of differentiation. In addition, if students have difficulty shifting from more traditional definitions of "fairness" to a perspective supported by differentiation, it's important for the teacher to be aware of that and understand what obstacles stand in the way of the class feeling fair to its members. This part of the conversation is worth exploring relatively early in the year and revisiting as the year evolves.

What will success in this class mean?

One of the seemingly immutable artifacts of "how we do school" is that success is typically defined in terms of a grade on a report card. Not only is that a *limited* view of success—it's a *limiting* one. There are students who make steady As on report cards with little effort or evidence of growth, and there are students who make low grades but have every right to cheer because they have demonstrated heroic commitment to learning and have grown remarkably despite falling short of a specified goal.

We'll discuss grading in differentiated classrooms in more detail later in this book. However, at some point relatively early in the year, it's important for the teacher to involve students in thinking about what it means to be successful in life—and in the classroom. This might be done by presenting students with brief biographies of two famous figures, one of whom gets lots of attention but makes little substantial contribution to anything worthwhile and one of whom devotes more attention to making a difference than to being in the spotlight. It might be done by having students compare two characters in a book or movie, one of whom has a harder life than the other but continues to work toward a goal in spite of the difficulties. It might be done through an example of two (unidentifiable) students—one in whom the teacher feels great pride despite the fact that the other student receives more accolades. It might be accomplished by sharing personal stories about times when students felt genuinely proud of themselves and other times when they knew they had little to be proud of in spite of praise from others. The point of this discussion is to raise the possibility that rewards—grades included—don't often reveal the whole story.

This is also a time to let students know that they are encouraged to think about success as having several parts. One is how hard and wisely a person works in order to grow. A second is how much a person grows. The third is whether a person reaches or exceeds a goal that required growth. Teachers should help students begin to develop and consider language that reflects these three markers of success. Students should also be assured that the teacher will be looking for a number of attributes and will ask them to look for these attributes in themselves, as well. Those attributes might include

- Hard work.
- Work habits that contribute directly to student success.
- Personal goals that require sustained work and attention.
- Willingness to take intellectual risks (i.e., to take a chance when something seems hard to do).
- Willingness to revise work to make it better.
- Willingness to seek help in order to grow and succeed with difficult tasks.
- Significant progress and substantial growth.
- Persistence in reaching or surpassing class goals.

Two principles that benefit learners and learning are that (1) working diligently and intelligently leads to growth, and (2) growth ultimately enables individuals to achieve and exceed most goals. This is the essence of a growth mindset—a fundamental underpinning of differentiation—and it is essential for genuine success. We fare best in the long term when we compete against ourselves rather than against other people.

Let students know that they will often hear you ask, "Is this the best *you* can do—the most *you* can give to this task?" Let them know that you hope they will join you in celebrating growth whenever it occurs for any student in the classroom.

None of the six questions explored in this chapter should be seen as "handled" during a single conversation (or a single year, for that matter). Teachers who lead students to develop a shared classroom vision that seeks to maximize growth for every student will help them continue to explore the questions and their relevance throughout the year and across years. Subsequent conversations may be short or long, individual or in a group, but they will be necessary for ideas about the classroom to "grow up" as the year progresses.

Teachers as Leaders of Parents in Understanding Differentiation

There are at least three important points to make about teachers who work effectively with parents to help them understand and contribute to a class that is focused on the success of each individual learner. First, it is important to realize the central role parents can play in helping a teacher know students better. Parents should always have greater *depth* of knowledge about their children than a teacher could ever hope to attain. On the other hand, teachers (at least after a few years in the classroom) have much greater *breadth* of knowledge about students of a particular age and in a particular subject than most parents. A wise teacher invites parents to contribute their depth of knowledge and, in turn, offers those parents a perspective on their children that is derived from a broad awareness of child development. It is a much better idea to proactively forge a mutually beneficial partnership than to allow an adversarial relationship to develop with parents. A teacher in a differentiated classroom simply needs help to know each student better, and most parents are a fantastic source of that information.

Second, it is critical for teachers to understand the role that culture plays in shaping parental response to school. This is particularly critical if parents are not from the majority culture. For example, parents from some cultural groups may feel uncomfortable if they think that they are being asked to tell the teacher how to teach; they consider it disrespectful of the teacher's competence. Parents from cultures that operate from a collectivistic (as opposed to an individualistic) perspective may be uncomfortable if their child seems singled out for praise, because their culture emphasizes the group over the individual. For the same reason, parents from collectivistic cultures may initially be more interested in hearing about their child's behavior in and contribution to the group than about grades and test scores (Rothstein-Fisch & Trumbull, 2008; Tomlinson, 2022). It is also extremely important to know that parents from all backgrounds care about and want to support the success of their children. Absence from parent meetings may have much more to do with a lack of transportation, childcare, or confidence with English than with personal attitudes about the importance of school. Teachers who are culturally competent invest in understanding the diverse cultures of their students, and they use that knowledge to build successful partnerships with both children and their parents.

Third, few parents argue with the baseline intent of differentiation if it is articulated clearly and in a way that is relevant to their desires and concerns. The fundamental message about differentiation from a teacher to a parent should be as follows:

- I am pleased that I will be teaching your child this year, and I want to do everything I can to help your child succeed.
- I have learned over the years that I am a better teacher when I understand students' particular strengths and needs as individual learners.
- I want to know what you value in terms of growth for your child this year so I can support development in those areas.
- I hope you will help me understand what some of your child's strengths and needs are as the year continues.
- My intent in class is to use what I can learn to help your child grow as much and as fast as possible to achieve and, in some cases, exceed the goals that are established for our class.

There are few parents who would respond, "I don't want you to know my kid, and I don't want you to help my kid learn as much as possible." What the philosophy and practice of differentiation aim to do is precisely what most parents want for their children—create a class in which a student is known and valued as an individual and where there is a reliable support system to build on the student's strengths, help shore up or circumvent weaknesses, and maximize academic growth for the time that the student is a member of the class.

Teachers can do the same activity with parents at a back-to-school night that they used to introduce differentiation to their students. As the year progresses, they should take every opportunity to communicate clearly and without education jargon that they are (1) working diligently to set clear and important goals for the class, (2) persistently following the progress of their students with regard to the goals, (3) providing clear feedback to the students to help them grow, and (4) using what they learn about students and their development to help them grow as far and as fast as possible. At every opportunity, teachers should also invite parents to share insights that will help them do their job better.

Be sure, however, that the emperor is wearing clothes. In other words, deliver what you promise. If a student is having difficulty reading or writing in 10th grade, do what's necessary to support the student's growth in that area—even if you are a math or science teacher. If you have a 3rd grader who has mastered 6th grade math, do what's necessary to help the student grow mathematically—even if that means you have to find new collaborators or learn more math. If we want parents to trust us, we have to earn their trust.

Teachers as Leaders of Colleagues in Understanding Differentiation

Teachers who lead for differentiation have an opportunity to lead colleagues, including other teachers and principals, as well as students and their parents. Accepting this opportunity can benefit both the teacher leader and their colleagues. Teachers have been criticized for engaging in "private practice"—for staying to ourselves, for not sharing our practice with other teachers, and for failing to learn from other teachers. Teacher leaders who share their work with differentiation take care not to convey the message that they are resident experts or that they have completed their learning about differentiation. Rather, the message is that the teacher is interested in sharing ideas with colleagues who will help them grow in their work. When you lead peers to an understanding of and contribution to differentiation, the potential opportunities and benefits are limitless. Here are some important points to consider:

- Coplanning or coteaching with colleagues who are language learning specialists, special education teachers, reading teachers, gifted education teachers, and media and technology specialists enriches the teacher's repertoire, extends learning support for students, integrates specialties into the regular classroom, and helps to forge teams that work across specialties on behalf of a wide range of students.
- Inviting colleagues who are or can be available to be a second pair of hands on occasions when you need another adult in your classroom can provide

necessary images of flexible teaching and learning for teachers who may want to address student variance but don't know how to begin.

• Working with colleagues to develop and share relevant knowledge about students' cultures and using that knowledge in instructional planning can help incorporate more cultural awareness into all classrooms.

• Planning differentiated lessons with grade-level or subject-matter peers is much more efficient than planning in a silo. It also allows teachers to contribute in their areas of greatest strength while they learn from others who have different strengths.

• Sharing pertinent insights about students with their teachers for the following year can give those teachers a more informed start and help them maintain a link with the previous teachers.

• Debating the merits of differentiation with other teachers can sharpen understanding and practice on both sides.

• Sharing ideas for differentiation with peers who want to address learner needs is both a gift and a relevant form of professional development.

• Providing staff development for peers can mute the voices that say, "Not in this school, not with these students." It can also show teachers how to begin addressing student variance, explain how to avoid pitfalls, and send the clear message that even teachers who seem ahead of the game still have room to grow.

If schools reflected a perfect world, every principal would be an informed advocate and supporter of classrooms that address the range of needs for every learner. Unfortunately, schools do not reflect (and are not in themselves) a perfect world. Principals work from the same limited understandings and conceptions of differentiation that virtually all other educators do, and many principals (and other administrative leaders) find it difficult to stay abreast of contemporary pedagogy. Even principals who have a fundamental understanding of differentiation and a sense that it's important to attend to students' varied learning needs may lack the appropriate depth of understanding and experience necessary to provide effective guidance and support for teachers to become confident and competent in implementing differentiation.

A teacher who is willing to be a leader of principals, specialists, supervisors, and other instructional leaders has the opportunity to benefit not only those individuals but also those colleagues who are affected by their practice. Consider the following insights that might result from conversations with or visits to the classroom of a teacher who is effectively differentiating instruction—insights that correct common misconceptions some administrators and supervisors have about differentiation:

- Students in a flexible classroom are focused on their work. Movement and conversation are purposeful. The classroom is orderly.
- Students who are disengaged in other settings often work with concentration in this class.
- Students have a greater level of independence and awareness about their work than in many other settings. When work is a good fit for students, discipline improves.
- Differentiation doesn't happen all day, every day; it occurs when a teacher applies what's been learned through observation and assessment about particular student needs.
- Student groups in a differentiated classroom are flexible, changing many times each day or week.
- In a differentiated class, students often use different paths to achieve common goals.

By inviting principals and other instructional leaders to observe and discuss differentiation, a teacher leader is likely to gain more support for their work while extending the administrator's capacity to support the work of other teachers in a more knowledgeable manner. In addition, of course, the questions and insights of an educator whose view of the classroom is somewhat different from the teacher's can stretch the teacher's thinking about differentiation as well.

Numerous educational experts (e.g., Fullan, 2001a; Marzano, 2009) remind us that strong leaders inspire their colleagues to look for solutions to challenges that have no easy answers and to realize that the degree of change needed to make our schools work as they ought to comes not from incremental adjustment but from bold new approaches. It is certainly the case that preparing an increasingly diverse student population to function with confidence at a high level in an increasingly complex world is just such a challenge. A teacher who leads for differentiation lives daily with that challenge; engages students, colleagues, and superordinates in confronting that challenge; asks the uncomfortable questions that necessarily surround it; and joins perspectives to find better solutions. When we meet the challenge, everyone benefits.

*   *   *

Part II of this book will address the more "practical" aspects of leading and managing for differentiation. It will examine some key aspects of what teachers in effectively differentiated classrooms *do* in order to enact what they *believe.*

Part II

Managing a
Differentiated Classroom

Contrary to common misperceptions, classroom management is not simply the process of arranging desks, rewarding good behavior, and choosing consequences for misconduct. Classroom management encompasses many practices integral to teaching, such as developing relationships; structuring classroom communities where students can work productively; organizing productive work around meaningful curriculum; teaching moral development and citizenship; making decisions about timing and other aspects of instructional planning; successfully motivating students to learn; and encouraging parent involvement.

—Pamela LePage, Linda Darling-Hammond, & Hanife Akar,
Preparing Teachers for a Changing World

The year begins and the students are in place. The teacher has the desire to know and teach them as individuals, along with a solid understanding of what high-quality differentiation is and why implementing differentiation improves the prospects of every student. The teacher is developing or fine-tuning meaningful learning targets, devising assessments that align with those targets, and creating relevant and engaging learning opportunities designed to connect students with important ideas and skills and to help them progress systematically to proficiency with the essential learning targets or goals (Erickson et al., 2017; Tomlinson, 2021; Tomlinson & McTighe, 2006; Wiggins & McTighe, 2005).

A central element in the teacher's thinking and planning is integrating differentiation into the fabric of the classroom (Sousa & Tomlinson, 2018; Tomlinson, 2014, 2017). The teacher has begun to issue an invitation to students to help create a classroom that is designed to work for each of them.

This sounds like a great start, and it is. However, it's only a start—a compass to chart a learning journey, not the journey itself. Even with these elements in reasonable working order and guided by a productively evolving philosophy, there's at least one more piece to the puzzle.

A teacher who has the best intentions, dynamic curriculum, and plans for differentiation cannot—and will not—move from compass to journey unless that teacher has the confidence to translate their ideas and plans into classroom practice. In other words, teachers who are uncomfortable with flexible classroom management will *not* differentiate instruction, even if they understand it, accept the need for it, and know how to plan for it. It is frightening for many teachers to risk trying new practices when they are uncertain of their readiness to do so, and fear prevents us from acting on knowledge. Strong leaders ensure that teachers are prepared to move from thought to practice, and that teachers understand their leaders believe that mistakes are both inevitable in making change and a sign of forward momentum (Fullan, 2008; Tomlinson & Murphy, 2015).

The chapters in Part II are intended to support teachers as they develop and extend their comfort level in this area. Part II, then, deals with the nuts and bolts of managing a learner-centered classroom, which, by its nature, requires flexible use of virtually every classroom element. This is a good place to distinguish again between classroom *management* and classroom *leadership*.

A teacher can manage a flexible schedule, earmark places to keep supplies, create designations that help students know which materials to access, craft a schedule for small-group instruction, develop ways to curb the noise that is a part of collaborative student work, and so on. However, that teacher must also lead students to understand and contribute to a differentiated classroom, overcome their fear of failure or challenge, invest in their own success, and cooperate with the routines that constitute classroom management. A teacher can manage these details without much of a philosophy. Real leadership requires an ethical compass regarding the responsibility of leadership, the value of those whom the leader asks to trust him or her, and the worthiness of the destination toward which the leader guides the group.

In Chapters 4–7, we'll describe many ways to proactively plan for potential "hot spots" in differentiated classrooms in order to develop a setting in which the teacher and students can work together to the benefit of each learner. Remember, too, that enlisting the trust of young people to be full participants in a differentiated classroom is a matter of leadership. Some students come to school with trust that school will work for them. Some come without that trust, generally because school has too often *not* worked for them. The teacher in a differentiated classroom understands the need to establish trust with individuals from *both* groups and aims to enlist the partnership of students from both groups in creating a classroom that will be a good fit for each of its members. The trust-building process does not follow a single timeline with every student. Some students fully intend *not* to trust teachers because of scars from the past. Still, a teacher who works from a philosophy that affirms the worth and capacity of every student moves forward in that process respectfully and patiently but persistently, taking care to be trustworthy all along the way.

As you read Part II of this book, ask yourself often how the concrete ideas presented will be shaped by your understanding of differentiation, your philosophy of teaching, and the degree to which you are able to share those underpinnings with your students. In other words, continue to think about the ways in which effective leadership and effective management in a differentiated classroom are interdependent.

4

Learning Environment
Setting the Stage for Academic Success

Learning occurs best in a positive environment—one that contains positive interpersonal relationships and interactions, that contains comfort and order, and in which the learner feels appreciated, acknowledged, respected, and validated.

—Barbara McCombs and Jo Sue Whisler,
The Learner-Centered Classroom and School

Few teachers argue with the following propositions:

- Some students require more time than others to achieve particular understandings or master particular skills.
- Some students bring with them to the classroom great reservoirs of knowledge that other students do not bring.
- Some students need to move around more than others.

- Some students speak a home language other than the language of the classroom.
- Some students seem to have given up on school—or on themselves or adults—and are angry or lethargic much of the time.
- Some students have difficulty concentrating during whole-class discussions and perform much better in small-group instruction.
- Some students have difficulty managing emotions or feelings.
- Some students are poor test takers but understand the content of the curriculum.
- Some students will not engage with learning if they fail to see the point of it.

The question is not whether teachers recognize that such differences exist in virtually every classroom, or even whether they impact student success. The question that plagues teachers is how to understand and address the differences they know exist.

The purpose of developing a differentiated classroom is to make sure that there's opportunity and support for each student to master critical knowledge, understanding, and skills as effectively and efficiently as possible. In other words, differentiation exists to "make room" for all kinds of learners to succeed academically. It also "makes room" for the teacher to support that academic success, which means they have the freedom to tailor instruction for individual students and small groups of students. Central to this process of making room for responsive teaching and student-focused learning is the creation of a learning environment that invites flexibility—in other words, a classroom where variability is the norm.

In fact, a flexible classroom is important to learning in general, not just to differentiation. Experts tell us that there are three categories of classrooms in terms of classroom management: *dysfunctional, adequate,* and *orderly.*

- *Dysfunctional* classroom environments are, of course, often chaotic. The teacher consistently struggles to maintain "control." Little sustained learning can take place.
- *Adequate* classroom environments exhibit a basic level of order, but the teacher still sometimes struggles to maintain it. Some sustained learning takes place.

• *Orderly* classroom environments fall into two further categories—*restrictive* and *enabling* environments. Orderly, *restrictive* learning environments are "tight-ship" classrooms. The teacher maintains a high degree of structure, manages routines tightly, and uses few instructional strategies. Orderly, *enabling* learning environments are found in smoothly running classrooms that manifest a looser (but not loose) structure. In these classrooms, teachers use a wide range of routines and instructional strategies, and the emphasis is on students making meaning of content (Educational Research Service, 1993).

In fact, researchers tell us, there is a direct relationship between a teacher's ability to manage a complex set of activities in a classroom and that teacher's ability to teach intellectually challenging material (LePage et al., 2005). This is because tasks that involve comprehension and problem solving require more flexibility than rote learning. When teachers are afraid of what might happen when students work independently, in small groups, with inquiry-oriented tasks, or at varied paces, they often opt to use more passive approaches to learning that effectually dumb down the curriculum. In those instances, teachers lower their expectations for students by using simpler modes of presentation and evaluation as a trade-off for classroom order. In other words, in those circumstances, teachers "teach defensively."

There are some sad and predictable cycles perpetuated by educators' perceptions that most students function best in tight-ship classrooms. One of those cycles stems from the reality that students often misbehave when the work they are asked to do is consistently too hard or too easy for them. Teachers in dysfunctional and adequate classrooms, as well as many who believe in the tight-ship model, necessarily persist in giving students tasks that are a poor fit for some of them (because differentiating requires flexibility, which threatens order). In turn, some students continue to be frustrated (and show it), which further reinforces the teacher's perception that to loosen the reins would be catastrophic. This conclusion, of course, simply feeds the frustration of many young people and, more to the point, serves them poorly.

A second regrettable cycle is an artifact from tracking practices in many of our schools. It is easy for educators to associate student behavior with student "ability." Unfortunately, students who misbehave are rarely seen as very bright (even though many of them are). There are certainly teachers who have grown comfortable with separating out students by "ability" and then teaching them in various tracks according to what "they can handle." Students who are frustrated by this mismatch, and who predictably act out as a result, are often placed in low-track classes (typified by low-level curriculum) that are run as tight ships or are either dysfunctional or adequate in terms of management. Conversely, students who comply with teacher directives are more likely to be seen as bright, and they are generally taught in orderly, flexible settings—that is, in classrooms where the emphasis is on understanding content and where teachers readily use a wide variety of instructional strategies to engage students with important ideas and skills (Cummings, 2020; Haberman, 1991; Hodges, 2001; Rosen, 2016; Spiegel, 2012).

Differentiation advocates teaching each student as an individual worthy and capable of handling a meaning-rich curriculum. It also advocates an environment in which each student comes to understand, own, and value their capacity as a learner. Doing so requires an orderly, flexible classroom environment. This chapter will focus on some key elements, guidelines, and strategies that enable teachers to create just such an environment.

Staging a Successful Drama

Think for a bit about a stage performance and the role of a good director. Successful directors don't simply buy scripts, put them in the hands of actors, give a few directions, and expect compelling results. In fact, much of the action behind a play that works happens *around* the script rather than *in* it. Along the way, a successful director must create affective and physical environments where the actors are supported in doing their best work so the play can evolve as it should.

En route to creating a play that works for an audience, the director must make it work for the actors. This happens on at least two levels. First, the director must come to know and understand each actor as an individual—the actor's strengths and vulnerabilities, preferred ways of working, and life experiences. It is upon these individual aspects that the director will draw as rehearsals progress. Not knowing these things would limit the potential impact of not only the actor but the director as well. To prepare, the director will likely do some background research on the actor before rehearsals begin. This will be followed by individual conversations throughout the rehearsal cycle and careful observation and reflection to understand what makes the actor shine as a character in some instances and what makes it difficult for the actor to bring a character to life in others.

In addition to learning to know and understand the actors as individuals, the director needs to help the actors move from being a collection of individuals to a cast, a troupe, an ensemble, a company—a team. They need to unify around a shared and commonly understood endeavor, without losing their distinctiveness. In other words, the director has to help build a sense of community among the actors so that the group works cohesively to benefit both individual and shared development. If the director is successful, the actors will develop valuable bonds during the production cycle. They will learn to pull together, support one another, cover for one another's shortcomings, and ultimately leave one another with both gratitude and sadness. Each individual will be stronger because of the group. The group will be stronger because of the individuals. Therefore, the director begins building an ensemble from disparate individuals when the actors arrive on day one—if not before. This work continues until the final curtain comes down.

Finally, in building an environment in which the actors can evolve, the director must create a physical context for the play. In the theater, of course, this is called a set. It is a miniature world designed on a small piece of real estate called a stage. It will contain whatever is necessary to make the play come to life and enhance the work of the actors. Nothing on the set is without purpose. From flats to props, everything contributes to the viability of the little universe. Shape, color, design, texture, and location are elements that sculpt the play and enliven the acting. When the set is ready, it is almost never final. Changes are nearly always made right up until opening night, and they will often continue throughout the life of the play.

The role of the teacher in developing an effective classroom environment is much like the role of the director. The drama, of course, is a compelling one—the interaction of individuals with ideas and skills that will change the individuals for better or worse. It requires risk, extreme effort, failure, self-awareness, honesty, small victories, and major triumphs. To make the drama work, the teacher must work quickly to get to know the actors and persistently to understand them. This means beginning early to build a team from a group of disparate individuals and continuing the team-building process for as long as the drama runs. In the small piece of real estate called a classroom, the teacher must offer a set in which the actors can work to make the play compelling. The remainder of this chapter will examine these three elements: getting to know students, building a community, and designing the physical environment of the classroom.

Getting to Know Students

An early and persistent quest for knowledge about students has at least four benefits.

1. It sends a message to each student that the teacher sees them as an individual, and it also suggests that they are interesting enough for an adult to want to know better. In this way, students begin to trust the teacher—to believe that the teacher will be an advocate and support system in the classroom—and start to shed the anonymity and alienation they might feel in the classroom.

2. It contributes to a student's willingness to do the difficult work of learning. Students work for people they value (i.e., people who value them).

3. It helps the teacher accept responsibility for the student's success. We invest most deeply in the people we really know—those with whom we have a relationship, those who are "three-dimensional" to us. It's difficult to let those individuals down.

4. It provides an open and continually expanding window into each student as an individual and a learner. Understanding a student's culture, likes and dislikes, personal sense of possibility as a learner, relationships with peers, home support, dreams, strengths and vulnerabilities, and preferred ways of learning makes it possible for a teacher to plan approaches to curriculum and instruction that have a higher likelihood of facilitating success for individual learners and for the class as a whole.

Teachers use an incredibly wide array of strategies to get to know their students as the year begins and to continue to learn about them as the year progresses. Let's consider a few examples.

Employing continual assessment

Continual assessment is central to the process of getting to know students in a differentiated classroom. There are several important points to keep in mind:

• Early in the year, develop ways to informally check students' mastery of essential skills and knowledge in your grade/subject. These essential skills include aural comprehension, visual comprehension, reading fluency, writing fluency, spelling, oral communication, and key academic vocabulary. These measures need not be exhaustive or time-consuming; for instance, you might generally assess spelling and writing fluency in a student's written response to an aural comprehension passage, or you might assess oral fluency while a student shares in a morning class meeting (younger students) or summarizes what they recall from yesterday's class (older students). Your perception of the student's proficiencies will progress over time, but it is nonetheless important to have a sense of where each student begins the year in terms of expected competencies—and to intervene as necessary to promote growth from the outset. Be alert to the likelihood that some students will appear to lack knowledge, skills, or understanding when the real problem is actually a barrier to revealing what they know. Some of these barriers include lagging language proficiency, attention challenges, anxiety, and difficulty with test taking and timed settings.

• Start fresh (but keep history in mind). Do not be overly swayed by a student's record from previous school years, comments from other teachers about the student, or standardized test data. The reason for this caution is to ensure that each student starts the year in your mind with all the possibilities necessary to move ahead and succeed. When a student becomes "that kid" who causes teachers to roll their eyes, who has "failed" the standardized test three years in a row, or who does poorly in science, it's difficult for the student's new teacher to have a growth mindset about that student. It's also difficult for that student *not* to be aware of doubts the teacher has about their prospects. Likewise, if you latch on to an image of a student as the one who is always on the honor roll or who is always at the top of the class on achievement tests, your mindset is likely to be "fixed" in regard to that student, and you will be less likely to challenge the student to see how far they can grow.

• Clarify the purpose of your information gathering and sharing. Students should understand that when you learn useful things about their interests, preferred ways of learning, and academic strengths and needs, you can use that information as you plan instruction. When you have insights about a student's work, be sure to share them with the student in a way that helps that individual work smarter and learn better. The goal is not for the teacher to become a "keeper of knowledge" about students, but to reflect that knowledge to students in ways and at times that give them more dominion over their own success. Consistently identify and celebrate what students can do rather than dwelling on their difficulties. Building on student strengths is a direct route to student motivation, buy-in, engagement, and achievement.

• Expect students to grow and change. Resist the inclination to assume that a student who is interested in insects in September will still be passionate about that topic in March. Some will; some will not. Also resist the inclination to categorize a student according to a particular approach to learning. Most people learn differently in different subjects, when content is new versus when it is familiar, and even at different times of day. Use the information you gain through observation to provide students with options, not to lock them into a predetermined kind of assignment. Check back with them often to see how they change and develop, and to help them understand and effectively use their options for learning and to express learning.

• Remember that students are your best source of information. Let them know you want to hear when things are going well—and when they aren't. Occasionally, use exit cards, checklists, digital surveys, end-of-unit evaluations, or other simple mechanisms to invite students to share their sense of how they're doing. Be sure to use what you learn. And bear in mind that students from some cultural groups *may* be more reticent to "advise" you for fear that doing so would be disrespectful. In those cases, don't push, but remind students that when they share ideas about how the class works best for everyone, it is helpful to you, and you appreciate their input.

A fundamental tenet of differentiation is that excellent teachers don't see themselves simply as teachers of content. Yes, they are fully committed to teaching content to young people, but learner-centered teachers understand that they must also be dedicated students themselves—of the content and of their students. They believe that teaching isn't complete until learning occurs, and that learning is predicated on a teacher's thorough understanding of both content and students.

Engaging in ongoing observation

An elementary teacher had her 4th graders play a "getting to know you" game in which they searched for classmates who had particular attributes (see Figure 4.1, p. 102). After the game, the teacher asked students to look at patterns in their classroom. She said, "Everyone who has an unusual pet, please come stand by me at the front of the room and tell us about your pet." She then said, "If you said you like helping out at school or home, raise your hand." To those students, she said, "Tomorrow, we'll begin to assign some important jobs in our classroom. I hope you'll consider signing up for one of those roles."

Figure 4.1
"Getting to Know You" Game

Name: _____

See if you can find at least one classmate who matches each category. When you find someone, write his or her name in the box for that category. See how many matches you can find before time is up.

I have three or more siblings.	I have been to more than two schools since 1st grade.	I can say a poem from memory.	I have a very unusual pet.	I have read at least one *Harry Potter* book.
I was born far away from here.	My birthday is on a holiday.	I am a good swimmer.	I like helping out at home and at school.	I can play a musical instrument.
I can make a basket from the free-throw line.	I have ridden a horse.	I enjoy drawing and painting.	I like to use a computer.	I can speak a language other than English.
I can whistle a song.	Someone in my family is a twin.	I can count backwards from 100 really fast.	I have won an award.	I am good at Double Dutch.

During the game and ensuing activity, the teacher took notes on her tablet and later alphabetized and accompanied her notes with photos of her students she'd taken with her tablet on the first day of school. She systematically added to the notes throughout the year as she observed students, talked with them, and generated pre-assessment and formative assessment information. She sometimes used these notes in conversations with students, and she sometimes used them in parent conferences—showing parents what she was learning and inviting them to contribute their own insights. She also regularly used them to plan lessons that were designed in response to her students' varied interests and needs. By the end of the school year, each student was represented by multiple data points and a "learner biography."

Going on home visits

A middle school science teacher in an urban area visited the homes of each of his students during the summer and early fall of the school year. If someone was home, he introduced himself, asked to say hello to his student, and explained that he was preparing to help students understand the ecology of their neighborhoods. He told parents that he was excited about getting to know their children and asked them to tell him a few things about the student that they thought were important for him to know. If no one was home, he left a printed note with much of the same information and told the parents that he wanted to personally invite them to visit him at school.

Mentally placing his students in a context helped him understand some important things about them even before they were in his classroom. Taking the time to visit their homes sent a clear message to parents and students that he wanted to know his students. It also indicated his understanding of the value of family in the lives of his students and in their learning. He continued to call and visit parents—most often with good news, but occasionally to talk with them about specific learning needs—throughout the year.

Creating unstructured and conversation spaces

A high school science teacher invited her students to use the classroom during a shared lunch period as a place to study, ask questions about their work, or just eat lunches they brought from home. The room almost always had 15–20 students in it during this period, which provided the teacher with an opportunity to see her students in a more relaxed atmosphere, to observe them with one another, and to provide assistance for them with reading, labs, and projects.

An English teacher colleague of this science teacher held monthly book club discussions at her home and encouraged students to come and share their ideas. Sometimes they discussed issues related to class assignments, but other times they reflected on topics of special interest to students or the teacher. The teacher always made a point of issuing special, private invitations to students she felt might be reluctant to come, and she always made sure they had safe, reliable transportation.

Attending extracurricular activities

The high school English teacher in the previous example also made it a point to attend at least one extracurricular event every other week so that she could see her students in voluntary settings. She tried to select events that would enable her to see the broadest possible swath of her students, but when two or more groups met simultaneously, she nearly always chose to attend the event in which her less academically engaged students participated.

Figure 4.2 (see p. 104) presents some additional ways of getting to know students. As noted, the purpose of each of these strategies is to help teachers teach

Figure 4.2
Strategies for Getting to Know Students

Strategy	Explanation
Greetings at the Door	In all grades and subjects, teachers can learn a great deal about students and greatly enhance communication by being at the door each day to speak briefly with each student as they enter the room. It is difficult to overstate the significance of asking specific questions (*How did the homework go last night?*), making personal comments (*You have new shoes on today*), and paying compliments (*I know the work was hard yesterday, so I appreciate that you stuck with it despite the difficulty*). The accumulation of information and interpersonal connections that result are immeasurable.
"All About Me" Bags	Students bring to school five objects that help the teacher and their classmates know them better. For very young students, it's a good idea to send a letter home so someone there can help them choose the objects and assemble the bag. Students can decorate their bags to show more about themselves if they'd like. Each day, the teacher asks three or four students to share their bags and the objects inside. Continue until everyone has had an opportunity to share.
Communication Journals	These are journals in which students write to teachers in a conversational way. There should be a secure place on the teacher's desk for students to place their journals when they write an entry they want the teacher to read. Students often write about what they do over the weekend, music they like, or suggestions they have for class. Occasionally, a student will write about a serious problem they want the teacher to know about. The teacher writes entries in response and then returns the journals. Communication journals provide the human-to-human exchanges that often are sadly lacking in class.
Note Taking	There is much to be learned from careful and systematic observation of students as they work in class. It is therefore useful for a teacher to carry a checklist of required skills, for example, and to spot check each student's work for evidence of those skills. It's also helpful to jot down general observations about individual students (along with the date) that can then be filed and arranged by subject area or class period. These observations form a growing archive of information on each student's learning development and needs.
Surveys	It's simple to develop surveys that ask students to share their sense of themselves as learners in a particular subject, their interests, and their methods for learning effectively. These surveys can be administered at the beginning of the year to jump-start teacher knowledge and as the year progresses to help teachers follow their students' development.
One to Ten	On a bulletin board, create a number line and label it 1 to 10. For younger students, draw an unhappy face over the 1 and a happy face over the 10. Title the board *How do you feel about _____?* The topic can change often; for example, one day students might be asked how they feel about a book they read yesterday in class, and another day they might be asked how they feel about starting a new math unit. Students then place paper dolls or name tags beneath the appropriate number to represent their feelings about that day's topic. This activity quickly illustrates the variety of feelings in the class on a particular topic, and it can also help determine the next steps in instruction. Over time, patterns will develop in individual students' responses.

more responsively through a deeper understanding of the individuals they teach. Teachers who are intent on knowing their students well use a variety of strategies throughout the year in service of that goal. It is useful, for example, to use student interests in forming expert groups, generating options for students to express learning, creating writing prompts or developing word problems that center on student interest, creating or selecting anchor activities (see pp. 154–155), generating analogies or examples to connect new learning with student interests, developing inquiries or individual explorations, seeking websites and gathering classroom materials for student use, creating exploratory learning centers, engaging in conversations with students, and so on.

Building a Community in the Classroom

A community is an outgrowth of people coming together around an opportunity to discover, recognize, appreciate, and reach toward some shared world. In differentiated classrooms, a teacher leads students to craft a common vision of a class in which there is room for everyone and individuals make a commitment to support one another in learning.

Being part of a community meets a fundamental human need for acceptance, belonging, affinity, respect, and caring. It reassures us that we can be part of something bigger than ourselves. For students from cultures with a collectivistic orientation, being part of a community is fundamental to how the world operates, and feeling a strong sense of "family" in the classroom provides normalcy and security (Rothstein-Fisch & Trumbull, 2008; Tomlinson, 2022).

Of course, not all communities are positive. Gangs and cults are examples of negative communities, but they still illustrate the basic need to be part of an identifiable circle of like-minded people who share a mission and provide one another with both an identity and a support system.

Teachers who lead students to craft a mutual vision of a differentiated classroom envision something like the democratic classroom described by James Beane (2005). In such places, student differences are not problems to be overcome, students are not separated according to their differences, and uniformity is not mandatory. Teachers in these classrooms send the signal that diversity is a strength that leads to a genuinely democratic community in which young people learn to live and work together. The teacher models, teaches, and expects all students to be respectful, empathetic, and inclusive with their classmates. While it is not reasonable to expect that every student will become the best friend of every other student, it is absolutely a precondition to learning that each student feel welcomed, seen, appreciated, and contributing (Boykin & Noguera, 2011; Kafele, 2021; Tomlinson, 2022).

Beane (2005) reminds us also that at the core of democracy are the related principles that people (1) have a fundamental right to human dignity; (2) have a responsibility to care about the common good, dignity, and welfare of others; (3) can see their own personal fate tied to the good of the group as a whole; and (4) have the intellectual and social capacity to work together to resolve issues as they arise. This is a high-minded vision—one on which the United States has based its aspirations as a nation. Enacting it is not easy, but it is important. In the classroom, as in the nation, this vision challenges and inspires us to continual self-improvement.

For students, these aspirations generally speak to a teacher's high expectations. Grappling with these goals prepares students for the world outside their classroom and requires them to take responsibility for their thoughts, actions, and reactions—both in their own work and as part of a team. Thus, being part of a sound community in a differentiated classroom addresses a fundamental human need for affinity with a group, which, in turn, leads to the higher goals of self-realization and contribution to a common good. These attributes are also nonnegotiables for achieving equity of access to genuinely excellent learning opportunities for students who are often marginalized in schools and society (Boykin & Noguera, 2011; Kafele, 2021; Tomlinson, 2022).

For the teacher, leading to develop a strong classroom community adds depth to teaching. It also increases learner motivation, self-awareness, and acceptance of responsibility. Ultimately, it provides a support system of learners that helps the teacher guide and maintain the effective operation of a classroom designed to operate flexibly and maximize the growth of each student.

Developing community

Leading students to form a positive sense of community, of course, is tightly linked to getting to know students. As a teacher shows interest in knowing individual students and treats them with respect, others notice. It becomes evident that, in that teacher's classroom, people matter, and there are opportunities for all students to learn about one another and work together. The class is also engaged in a conversation about creating an environment in which each person is seen as valuable and in which the growth of each person is of ultimate importance. As the conversation unfolds, the teacher continues to bring students back to the original reason for creating a classroom that is responsive to each student—each student matters. Often implicit (but occasionally explicit) in this conversation is the idea that, in this classroom, "this is who we are; this is what we do." As a result, the group becomes more defined, and students eventually develop a better understanding of one another, see their ideas enacted, and work together with increased effectiveness. Over time, a community coalesces.

As is the case with getting to know students, there are many ways to contribute to the formation of a classroom community in which individuals share common interests and goals. Consider the following classroom examples.

A high school English teacher came to the honest but difficult conclusion that by the time students reached her class, few had a burning desire to read more poems, complete more grammar exercises, or write additional formulaic essays. She understood that she would have to create a classroom in which students felt connected in a way that made her content seem important to them. She began by creating a classroom space in which students could carry on a conversation. She told students small stories from her life, and she invited them to tell their own. "I love a good story," she often said. "I'll even delay a test for five minutes if someone has a good story to tell… but it better be good!" In time, she began to tell stories from her life that had more meaning. By then, her students were listening to one another with positive regard, and they trusted that they could share meaningful stories from their own lives. She helped them recognize how their stories were like those of the authors they read. She also helped them believe that their stories were worth preserving in written form. Throughout the year, she purposefully and simultaneously led students to bond around storytelling and related the material she taught to the people she taught. The class was life-shaping for her students; many of them developed into devoted readers and writers (Tomlinson & Doubet, 2005).

A primary teacher reserved a classroom wall to post 10 calendar pages—one for each month the students were in school. The pages were large and offered ample room to write. On the first day of school, she told her students that they would be writing a class history as the year went on. "When something important happens," she said, "we'll put it on our calendar with words and drawings and pictures. That way, we can all go back and read our history as a class." Each day, as school was about to end, she'd ask students to say what had been most important that day. Early in the year, she'd sometimes prompt students with "Here are three things that seem to be important today. Is there something else you can add to that list?" She made sure to include special moments in individual students' lives (that were shared that day) and whole-class items, including both positive reinforcement (e.g., "Everyone worked extra-hard with math today") and room for improvement (e.g., "We have to figure out how to talk more quietly when we work"). Students predictably followed her modeling as they made their own suggestions for the class history. Sometimes, the teacher added photos or students provided illustrations to go with their words. As the year progressed, students began to do more of the writing on the calendar. When adults came into the room, the teacher would ask volunteers to explain the calendar and several items they felt clearly showed what the class was like. (Students nearly always showed their parents the calendar when they visited the classroom.) Increasingly, the calendar became a shared story of "who we are," "what we do," and "why our work is important."

A middle school math teacher saw that her students were sometimes frustrated by the challenging math they were studying. One day, she offered a "jeer" for the group—a cheer with a grumpy personality. She invited students to chant the jeer with her three times in succession, with each rendition louder than the one before. When they finished, she said, "Here's our new slogan: *We gripe and conquer!*" She was surprised how the moment changed the tone in the classroom. Students vented, laughed, and worked with much less tension and hesitation than in days past. A few days later, when she noticed frustration building again, she said, "Who remembers the jeer? I think we need to practice it again." On another day, she said, "OK, time for a jeer, but I'm getting tired of that old one. Anyone have a fresh idea?" Students began to bring in "anti-math" jeers for the class, and she used them when needed. Each time, she followed the class chants with the question "What's our class motto?" The students responded in unison, "We gripe and conquer," and they did. The jeers were one of many techniques the teacher used to bring her students together as conquerors of math, rather than victims of it. Students routinely came back to visit the teacher after they graduated, and they inevitably told her that they remembered the lesson she taught them: It's OK to get frustrated, but it's not OK to give up.

A high school French teacher put a cupcake on a student's desk on his birthday. She stood by the student's desk as class began, wished the student a happy birthday, and acknowledged two or three things about him that she particularly valued. The rest of the students applauded and class went on. The importance of this small gesture might be easy to overlook. However, it was evidenced by a quiet student in the class who had an opportunity to travel abroad with her parents later that year. This student was very excited about the trip because she would have a chance to speak French and bring some things back for the class. Shortly before the trip, though, she told her mother she couldn't go and asked her to get a refund for her ticket. The mother, puzzled and not very pleased, asked her daughter why she suddenly felt she couldn't go on the trip. Her daughter replied, "I didn't realize the trip was during the week of my birthday. I'd miss my cupcake in French. I have to be there for that!" It wasn't the cupcake that the student would miss, of course; it was the teacher's public acknowledgment of her value and what it communicated to the class that made the day more important than the trip. The cupcake ritual modeled an ethic of respect and appreciation that pervaded everything in the classroom. It was one of many ways the teacher led the students to conclude, "This is who we are, and this is how we treat one another in here."

Teachers develop their own strategies to identify and clarify the specific goals to which they aspire as a class. In doing so, they not only clarify what matters most in the classroom, but they also help students come together around those significant ideas. They emphasize community not in lieu of content but rather as a means of opening students to the learning process. Figure 4.3 features more examples of methods teachers can use to build a more positive classroom community.

Figure 4.3
Strategies for Building a Classroom Community

Strategy	Explanation
Purposeful Talk	Teachers in many elementary classrooms use morning meetings to provide time for students to greet one another, set a tone, plan ahead, reflect, model behaviors, and so on. These meetings allow teachers to spotlight things that matter to individuals and to the group. They also allow students to hear and respond to one another, thus defining what matters most in the classroom and what will come to define the community. Teachers in middle and high school classrooms make similar use of very brief segments of time at the beginning or end of class to share anecdotes, reflect on what recently transpired in class, plan for what's ahead, and be reminded of the ideas they are working to implement in their classroom.
Keeper of the Book	Students take turns keeping notes (in a notebook or on the computer) to log what is taking place during a particular class, directions for projects, assignment deadlines, and so on. If a student is absent or just uncertain about the reason for a task, task requirements, or criteria for success, the logbook will provide support and guidance. Students support one another's success in this way and also learn to take pride in the quality of their entries when it's their turn to be "keeper of the book."

(continued)

Figure 4.3—(*continued*)

Strategies for Building a Classroom Community

Strategy	Explanation
Integrating New Students	Current students in a class make plans to welcome and integrate new students—they decide what is necessary to make sure new students feel welcomed and are ready to join the class in the work they are doing. Students accept various roles in this process, and the class debriefs throughout the year to continue to enhance their plans.
Welcoming Guests to the Classroom	Students play an active role when parents, other teachers, administrators, or community members come to their classroom. Depending on the nature of the guest and visit, students make sure guests are welcomed, have a place to sit, have copies of student assignments, observe or participate in student conversations, and receive explanations about the nature of the classroom community. Students can play different roles in the process, and roles can change over time. In a differentiated classroom, students should quickly be able to explain and illustrate the classroom philosophy and practice for guests.
Working on a Sustained and Meaningful Product	Students in elementary school can build a model of their community throughout the year, or they can establish communication with or raise funds for other students of their age in a part of the world they are learning about. Middle school students can study the developmental needs of young children while they examine award-winning children's books as a way to understand the elements of literature. Ultimately, they can write and illustrate a library of books for primary students in a feeder school, read their books to those students, and lead discussions on the books. High school students can develop and publish a science magazine for elementary or middle school students that relates important science concepts to the personal interests of those students. This kind of meaningful, sustained product brings students together around a common purpose.
Modeling What Matters	It's essential for all teachers to model classroom behaviors they want their students to exhibit. This means listening respectfully to each student's ideas and questions, demonstrating positive regard for student differences, complimenting legitimate student accomplishments, politely but firmly rejecting behaviors that undermine the efforts of anyone in the group, and so on. Students need to see their teachers also use these principles as they work with colleagues and associates in the school.
Teaching the Skills of Collaboration	Young people learn most important skills through a combination of teaching and doing. Thinking about the age/development of their students and the nature of the work those students will do collaboratively, the teacher can determine which skills to teach prior to given assignments, which to teach as students are working, and which will need ongoing focus for much or all of a school year. Skills that support collaboration include empathy, listening carefully, respect, appreciation of diverse perspectives, organization, goal clarity, communicating clearly, adaptability, asking fruitful questions, giving actionable feedback, evaluating progress, supporting group members in learning (versus doing the work for them), contributing to group success, acknowledging the contributions of others, and apologizing when necessary.

Using student groups and classroom community

In differentiated classrooms, the use of student groups is integral to building a productive, positive community, but it's not the only requirement. In fact, effectively differentiated classrooms will inevitably also require students to work independently and in whole-class sessions. Theoretically, at least, it might be possible to differentiate without ever having students work in small groups. Except for concerns about classroom "control," however, it's difficult to understand why a teacher would want to do that.

When student groups function effectively, they are highly motivating to students. They provide an opportunity for students to share ideas, get input, encounter alternative ways of approaching problems or tasks, and get support. For many students, this is a precursor to successful learning. Groups also make the classroom more efficient for teachers, who can, for example, more effectively focus on five or six groups than on 30 individuals. In Chapter 6, we'll look at procedures for helping students work effectively in groups. Here, though, we'll spotlight some principles of effective grouping that support the beliefs and practices of differentiation.

Use flexible grouping. A nonnegotiable aspect of effective differentiation is that teachers plan a consistent flow of varied student groupings within a unit of study based on the nature of the work and the individual needs of students. This allows students to see themselves and one another in a variety of learning contexts, and it provides the teacher with regular opportunities to observe each student in multiple contexts. For example, Benjamin may be scheduled to work four days this week with peers who have similar readiness levels and skill needs. However, the teacher's plan for literacy groups during the week should also, for instance, include opportunities for Benjamin to share some reading with students who have similar interests regardless of their readiness needs, to work with another group of students who choose to express what they learn in a particular format, to work independently at a center, and to work with a student of his choice to discuss class material. At other times in the day, Benjamin is likely to work with turn-and-talk groups, think-pair-share partners, an inquiry group, a brainstorming group, and so on. Students perform and learn differently in different circumstances; they deserve the opportunity to work with varied peer groupings on a regular and consistent basis so they can see themselves, and be seen by others, as multidimensional learners. Flexible grouping is an indispensable tool for ensuring equity of access to powerful learning opportunities for each learner in a class, as it supports student awareness, appreciation, and contribution of the full spectrum of peers in their class (Doubet, 2022).

Teach up. Design group tasks to ensure that each student works with a rich curriculum to think about and apply essential ideas and skills. All students will need time to practice a discrete skill or work with a knowledge set, but there should not be student groups that consistently practice skills out of context while other group tasks cast students as thinkers, problem solvers, and creators. Begin by planning tasks that challenge advanced learners, and then scaffold as needed for learners who are not yet as advanced. Teaching in this way is an indicator of a growth mindset teacher, and it will increase the prospects, self-image, and achievement of virtually all learners. We'll look at teaching up in greater detail later in the book.

Use multiple-ability tasks. Such tasks have more than one right answer or way to solve a problem, are intrinsically interesting and rewarding to a variety of students, allow different students to make different contributions to the successful completion of a task, and require a variety of skills and strengths for successful completion (Cohen & Lotan, 2014). Multiple-ability tasks often draw on a variety of media because of their high relevance to students, the access they provide to important content, and the opportunities they allow for students to express learning. These tasks also emphasize the critical importance of reading and writing to student success while they extend to students a greater range of learning modes and expression modalities.

Assign (or let students select) essential roles within groups. Individual roles indicate that each student has a genuinely important academic or intellectual contribution to make to the task. For example, if one student in a group is designated as the reader and another as the timekeeper, it's evident to students that the reader has a more "valuable" role than the timekeeper. On the other hand, if one student is expected to diagram the steps necessary to solve a math problem, another is expected to write prose directions for solving it, and a third student is responsible for using manipulatives or other objects to explain the thinking behind the solution, each student contributes equally to the task of "demonstrating what a student who has been absent this week would have to know, understand, and be able to do in order to feel competent with the kind of math problem we've been focusing on this week." Groups in which only some members demonstrate competencies critical to success create a sort of caste system of winners and losers rather than contributing to a sense of community in the classroom.

Make content accessible to everyone. When students work together in groups (just as should be the case when they work independently), ensure that the important content is accessible to everyone in the group. English language learners, for example, should have a feasible method for bridging their two languages. It can be useful, for instance, to place a student who is new or relatively new to the language of the classroom in a group with a student who speaks the same home language as the new English learner but who is further along in reading and speaking in English and who therefore can serve as a bridge for the newer learner. To address a wide range of reading proficiencies in a mixed-readiness group, one student can be designated as the group's reader. Text or directions can be recorded, or students can read materials at different levels of complexity or in students' varied languages, and then the group members can work together on a common task. Offering video and audio sources of content can also be a game-changer for students with a range of reading challenges.

Assign competence. Observe students carefully, noting the particular strengths, skills, and insights they bring to group work. When you see a worthy and honest contribution, remark on what you saw. For example, you might say, "I think the question Sherisa just asked was a significant one. It caused you to rethink the line of logic you were using as a group. The ability to ask a challenging question at the right time is a very useful skill." It's important for all students to receive this sort of affirmation, but it's particularly important for students who may be seen as having lower status among their peers to hear—and for their peers to hear—such comments from a teacher when they are genuinely warranted (Cohen & Lotan, 2014).

Effective use of instructional groups benefits individual students in terms of their academic development. It also contributes to a sense of classroom community as students consistently have opportunities to work with a broad range of classmates on a variety of tasks designed to ensure that everyone is a meaningful contributor to the shared assignment.

Designing a Physical Environment to Support Learning

As is the case with all other classroom elements, the goal of planning the physical environment of a classroom is to maximize equitable and high-quality opportunities for teaching and learning. To that end, the physical environment in a differentiated classroom should provide the structure and predictability young people need in order to feel secure. In addition, it should allow flexibility to attend to both group and individual needs in the context of a rich, meaning-focused curriculum.

In very much the same way that a person is represented by their choice of clothing, hairstyle, or music, a classroom's environment communicates a good bit about what that classroom is about. It speaks subtly, or not so subtly, about the nature and philosophy of the teacher, the degree of organization that's likely to characterize the classroom, and the teacher's concern for students, their comfort, and their success.

We'll briefly examine three elements that teachers should consider carefully as they contemplate classroom arrangements. Decisions regarding each element will contribute to or detract from a focus on learning. A classroom does not have to be "upscale" to be thoughtful, organized, and flexible; nor does it have to be "upscale" to communicate the seriousness with which the teacher considers the success of each learner.

As we have suggested, a differentiated classroom is student focused. It therefore carries the expectation that *students* will meet the following objectives:

- Increase their proficiency and comfort while working independently, in small groups, and as a whole class.
- Think at high levels—they will comprehend and apply what they learn.
- Support the learning of their peers actively and effectively.
- Help the teacher make the classroom work for each member of the class and the class as a whole.

Further, a differentiated classroom carries the expectation that the *teacher* will do the following:

- Study students consistently in order to teach them more effectively.
- Build a community in the classroom intentionally and explicitly.
- Work with individuals, small groups, and the whole class on a regular basis.
- Use flexible student groupings.
- Address the readiness, interest, and learning preference of each individual learner.

Furniture arrangement and floor plan

We can make some decisions about a classroom's furniture arrangement and floor plan that directly support the student and teacher expectations noted above.

Two useful questions that teachers should ask when they think about furniture arrangement and floor plan are "What are all of my options?" and "Which of my options best align with the goals I have for myself and my students?" Here are some guidelines to consider as you think about your classroom's furniture and floor plan:

- Choose options that support collaboration. When possible, opt to use tables—or tables and individual desks—instead of individual desks only. Straight rows of desks do little to invite or facilitate meaningful collaboration. If new furniture is not an option, many schools and districts have storage areas full of furniture that is no longer used. Discarded tables can be covered easily with poster board or heavy construction paper then decorated with contact paper or painted in bright colors to make the best-looking furniture in the school.

- Provide space for individual learning. Consider arranging four to eight individual seats or desks in one area of the room. Despite the general desirability of tables over individual desks, this sort of "independent study" area can be useful for students who need to work alone on a particular assignment, who are having a bad day, who have been absent and need to make up work, or who struggle with emotions and need to have some time away from peers.

- Arrange the room so that you can easily walk among students. This is essential for students to feel your presence and for you to observe students while they work. It also allows you to reach each student easily when they require assistance.

- Consider your students' needs and preferences. As much as possible, arrange student seating areas (including carpet seating for young learners) in a way that accounts for individuals' responses to "private space." When students are seated too close to one another, some begin to feel threatened. Others simply take advantage of the opportunity to "reach out and touch someone," which can create unnecessary problems. On the other hand, some students benefit from physical proximity to peers as they work. As with most other elements, planning for flexibility to address a variety of needs is essential.

- Position your desk in an out-of-the-way place instead of front and center. The latter option takes up much valuable real estate and puts the emphasis in the wrong place. In an effectively differentiated classroom, a teacher's desk will be used very little!

• Plan multiple furniture arrangements. The ideal classroom arrangement is one that supports varied tasks and is beneficial for whole-class discussions, small-group work (pairs, triads, and quads), and individual work. Post the floor plans and teach students how to move the furniture into the various arrangements in an orderly way. See page 153 for additional details.

• Plan one arrangement that encourages student-to-student discussion. This would likely be in the shape of a *U*, a circle, or two semicircles that face each other. Straight and orderly rows of desks that face the teacher are better suited to an adult talking at students rather than students talking and listening to one another. With younger students, this need is often met with a designated space where everyone sits on a rug to listen to directions or share ideas.

• Don't forget about accessible storage. Try to line a significant portion of the room with shelving, cabinets, cubbyholes, mailboxes, or other structures that allow you to house a variety of materials, supplies, and artifacts. Look for discarded shelves if necessary, and get students to help paint them. Shelves made from bricks, cinder blocks, and board planks also work just fine!

• Think about the location of "specialty" areas, such as science lab space, listening stations, computer centers, and learning/interest centers. If these areas will be set up most (or all) of the time, and if students will need to use them independently or in small groups, they should be clearly visible to you at all times but out of sight for students who are not using them.

• Include a "Peace Corner" or a "Zen Zone." Set up a space that any student can go to work, reflect, or regroup, alone and away from conversations or tensions. A quiet zone is often tremendously helpful for students who need it—and for the classmates around them too!

Wall space and bulletin boards

These environmental elements serve a dual purpose. They can humanize a classroom, and they can also contribute considerably to learner independence and success. The stereotypical classroom image tends to be of blank walls and bulletin boards filled with cutout images from teacher stores—which, of course, do little to facilitate student success or make the class seem more learner oriented. Consider the following suggestions when you think about wall space and bulletin boards in the classroom:

• If using student group or assignment charts, be sure to reserve a large and prominent place to post them. Make certain they are large enough for students to see from anywhere in the room.

• Designate some wall or bulletin board space that will predictably contain information about key assignments—for example, criteria for success, suggested resources, due dates, and reminders.

• Consider creating a "hint board," "hint cards," or an intranet site to collect reminders of how to do things that students need to know but may have forgotten. For example, if students learned about haiku poetry last month and will now write a haiku to express their feelings about something they are studying in science, the hint board/cards might contain the elements of haiku in addition to a few illustrations. Hint boards and cards help students work more independently and thus preserve teacher time to work with individuals and small groups. Figure 4.4 illustrates examples of material that might be included on hint cards: formulas, procedural steps, examples, maps, and so on.

Figure 4.4
Examples of Hint Cards

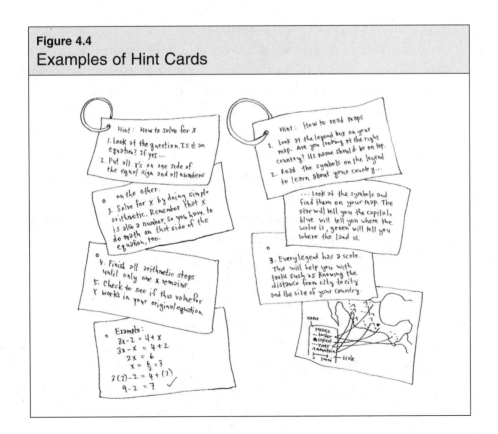

• Designate space for a few exemplars of high-quality student work from past years for assignments this year's students are currently doing. In a differentiated classroom, there may need to be exemplars at varied levels of complexity for a single assignment—differentiated by readiness or by options for different modes of expression through which students can express their learning. All exemplars, however, should meet the criteria for success. This area should also contain rubrics and annotations or other means of helping students see *why* posted exemplars are, in fact, exemplary.

• Designate space that will feature attractively posted, frequently changing examples of high-quality student work (both individual and group work) that this year's students have recently completed. Take care to point out instances in which student work exhibits significant growth as well. Guide students in using exemplars as tools for understanding and developing their own work.

• Designate some wall space that can intentionally remain blank. Use this area to create a working space for students who may be distracted by visual stimulation and who will concentrate better if they look at "plain" walls.

• Try to find wall space, bulletin board space, or shelf space where you and your students can place objects or materials that are personally interesting, or where students and student achievements can be featured. Figure 4.5 provides one teacher-developed example of a space that features students throughout the year. The middle school teacher who developed this idea uses one bulletin board to spotlight five students each week. She teaches approximately 150 students, and every month she asks approximately 20 students to complete a "Here's Somebody Who" template about themselves along with a few relevant photos. (Preparing the board takes very little time since students do most of the work.) She asks students to mount their templates and photos on bright cardboard, and when it is time to change the displays, she returns the previous ones and encourages students to give their displays to a parent, grandparent, or someone else important to them. She adds, "Please tell them that I'm grateful for the opportunity to teach you." The board has been very popular with all of her students, and most students enjoy reading about their peers who are featured.

Materials, supplies, and organizers

Just as the appropriate use of furniture, floor space, and wall space is critical to facilitate learner success and support flexibility in the classroom, careful

---

Figure 4.5
"Here's Somebody Who" Bulletin Board

Here's somebody who...

Likes _____

Really likes _____

Really, really likes _____

Doesn't like _____

Really doesn't like _____

Really, really doesn't like _____

Has changed from _____ to _____

Is proud of _____

Wishes people knew _____

Is willing to work hard for _____

Dreams about _____

Will someday be _____

Is already _____

Whose name is _____

---

planning for placement of materials, supplies, and organizing elements can also help achieve these goals. The idea is to give students access to what they will need as they work in a way that maximizes efficiency and minimizes disruption. By preplanning these elements with student success in mind, teachers contribute to each student's sense of both individual and group competence. Consider the following suggestions when you think about materials, supplies, and organizers in the classroom:

• Store materials and supplies that will be used often (e.g., books, paper, markers/crayons, rulers, lab supplies, learning games, manipulatives, headphones) in places where students can access them easily—without having to walk through work areas—and in view of the teacher. If necessary, use more "remote" areas of the room for materials or supplies that students will use less often or that fewer students will use.

• Store materials and supplies that should be unavailable to students in places that are difficult for students to see or access—for example, high shelves or cabinets, file cabinets, or a storage area behind the teacher's desk. Be sure to designate these areas as off-limits to students. These materials might include equipment the teacher will need, supplies for upcoming units, or materials that will be used by a few students with specific needs at some time during the year.

• Use bins, tubs, or boxes where possible to keep supplies organized and neat rather than having them spread out on tables or shelves.

• Designate and label places in the room where students will turn in class-work and homework as they complete it. In elementary classrooms, where teachers teach multiple subjects, it makes sense to have different boxes or trays for each subject. Use icons and color-coding to help students know where to place their work if they are just learning how to read, have a learning disorder, or are English language learners.

• Have students use file folders to organize work that is "in process" (e.g., checklists of completed work, mastered skills, books read). It's helpful to color-code these folders for secondary classes where teachers have multiple classes. For example, write students' names on the folders in blue for first period, green for second period, and so on (note that it's even more helpful to use folders of five different colors). It's also useful to have color-coded boxes or crates for each class from which folders can be retrieved and to which they can be returned. For classrooms in which students use a shared digital platform, some of these organizational practices will take place online. It is still helpful, however, for the classroom to have an organizational system that enables students to work directly and tangibly with varied materials, examples, and supports.

• Designate a place in the room where students will go to find anchor activities.

• Have more than one pencil sharpener and trash can in the classroom, and make sure they are in locations that are easily accessed with minimal distraction for other students, or provide sharpened pencils in a cup or box so students don't need to use the pencil sharpener. Used pencils work just fine!

Decisions about the use of furniture, floor space, wall areas, bulletin boards, materials, supplies, and classroom/digital organizers will vary somewhat among grades, subjects, and schools and with the confidence of the teacher. It is *not* the case, however, that these issues are relevant only to the lower grades. From preschool through high school, the most effective teachers make judicious use of every resource at their disposal to maximize their own—and their students'—efficiency and effectiveness.

In Chapters 5 and 6, we'll look at ways in which classroom routines allow flexibility and extend academic growth. Chapter 5 examines routines that prepare students to work in a differentiated classroom, and Chapter 6 examines routines that are important once students begin to work in a differentiated classroom.

5

Classroom Routines
Preparing for the Work Ahead

As with all other human characteristics, learning is diverse and different for each learner. It is a function of heredity, experience, perspectives, backgrounds, talents, interests, capacities, needs, and the unpredictable flow of any particular life. . . . It is exactly this diversity that provides innumerable opportunities for expanding learning—first, by acknowledging differences in physiological, personal, linguistic, cultural, and social backgrounds, and second by focusing on the common features that make all of us human. But the differences must be taken into account as well to provide all learners with the necessary opportunities for learning and self-development.

—Lorna Earl, *Assessment as Learning*

Classroom procedures and routines are prescribed ways of doing things that allow teaching and learning to proceed in a structured, predictable, and efficient manner. Their purpose should be clear to both teacher and students: they exist to help students learn as effectively as possible. They are methods to build student competence with content and as learners, not mechanisms to control students. Paradoxically, the presence of stable, predictable routines is what creates the flexibility individual students need to keep growing at the pace that's right for them.

The Basics

Regardless of the procedure or routine, there are important steps that teachers must follow.

Determine them. What routines need to be established in the classroom for things to run smoothly and for everyone to learn and grow? The number of routines will vary with students' age, the nature of the class, and your comfort level as a leader of students. Don't try to prescribe a routine for everything students do. Micromanaging is tedious for everyone and quickly sends the message that you don't trust students and are trying to manage them rather than help them manage the details of learning. On the other hand, there should be clear routines for processes that are fundamental to the operation of the class and essential for student success, such as starting class, getting and replacing materials and supplies, and monitoring classroom noise level.

Clarify the rationale for them. Be sure to help students understand both the general rationale for a routine (e.g., so the classroom can work for everyone, so everyone can succeed as a learner, so everyone can concentrate on their work) and the specific rationale for a particular routine (e.g., a neat, orderly, and organized classroom helps all students easily find the things they need to get their work done, and I spend less time cleaning and more time helping students).

Develop them. Sometimes, it makes good sense for a teacher to say, "Here's how we need to do this…." This is certainly true with very young students, with students who lack structure in their lives, and when there is really only one acceptable way to proceed (e.g., when working with potentially hazardous materials in a science lab). On the other hand, when students can reasonably help a teacher develop a procedure, it builds student ownership of the ideas, student investment in making the procedures work, and student–teacher partnerships in making the entire classroom work. In either case, be sure the individual steps in the procedure are clearly delineated and understandable to everyone. In some instances, this may mean posting the procedure for a time or giving it to students in a handout.

Teach them. Teachers know the importance of methodically teaching content, but we sometimes assume we can just tell students what a procedure is and they'll get it. Whatever we want students to learn, we need to teach (unless we have evidence that they already know it). Teaching a routine might mean that students literally practice the routine. For younger students, it might mean that you need to model the routine so they can see what it looks like when done correctly. It might mean students review the steps aloud and from memory. Whatever it takes for students to know, understand, and be able to smoothly carry out the routine is what you need to do. Teach routines as carefully and explicitly as you would teach a mathematical operation, a comprehension strategy, or the steps to write a five-paragraph essay.

Apply them. Have students begin using the routine in their work. Ask them to recall the reason(s) for the routine, its steps, and how it should look and sound as it is implemented.

Automatize them. In truth, a routine is a procedure that has become automatic—in other words, it's a procedure that is routine! To help students automatize a routine, use that routine repeatedly in a relatively short period of time.

Reflect on, revise, and review them. It's always important to observe students as they use a routine, take notes about the process, and reflect on the degree to which the routine is contributing to effective and efficient teaching and learning. Again, it sometimes makes sense to say, "Yesterday, I noticed that several students were having difficulty getting the help they needed while I was working with a small group. Today, I'm going to have two 'experts of the day' available instead of just one. Let's see if that makes things smoother for you." On the other hand, it can be very powerful for a teacher to work with students to reflect on how well a procedure worked. They can then engage the students to revise the procedures as needed. Students often understand a problem before the teacher does, and they nearly always have insightful suggestions about how to make things operate more smoothly. It's important to review routines from time to time to maintain clarity of understanding and consistency in application. This can be particularly useful after vacations or when students have not used a particular routine for a while.

It makes sense to let the routines evolve in a way that feels comfortable to both teacher and students. Some teachers will introduce most or all of their standard routines during the first week of school, and their students will follow the routines comfortably and proficiently within a few days. Others will practice one routine for several days before introducing another. The unique nature of both the teacher and students will set the pace. In general, however, it is a good idea to invest time in teaching and implementing routines as early in the year as possible. This prevents students from learning one way of "doing business" early in the year only to have to unlearn it as the year continues. Successfully enacting the routines fundamental to a classroom is necessary to create an orderly, flexible classroom that supports both complex thinking and differentiation. Students will benefit from working in this sort of environment as soon as it's feasible for them to do so.

Classroom Rules to Live By

Working with students at the beginning of the year to establish classroom rules, guidelines, or agreements is useful for several reasons. First, developing the rules can either lead to or reinforce the fundamental tenets of differentiation. Second, when a teacher asks the class to reach a consensus about the rules by which the group will live, it sends a distinct message that the teacher trusts the students to have good judgment. Third, as students discuss and listen to one another's ideas, a general tone and specific procedures begin to emerge for what it means to think and solve problems as a group. The evolution of community begins.

Some educators, however, make a reasonable argument for *not* establishing classroom rules. Generally, their sense is that a list of rules is unnecessary when curriculum, instruction, and learning environment work as they should—and that when they don't work as they should, a list of rules can't fix what's wrong. While there's truth in this perspective, it's also the case that crafting a set of guidelines for living and working well together is fundamental to a democracy and establishes a baseline for everything that will follow. Our persuasion is that a brief set of guidelines, operating principles, or rules can provide a sense of direction for the class and a touchstone for later discussions about the nature of the class and its goals. Such a set of guidelines can also provide the rationale for basic classroom procedures and routines. They should also, in our opinion, point to an intrinsic and positive (rather than extrinsic and punitive) way of operating in the classroom.

The following examples of classroom rules or guidelines have several things in common. They are brief. They are positive in tone. They challenge students. And they transfer into the world beyond the classroom door.

- Be nice.
- Work hard.
- No shortcuts.
- No excuses.

A middle school teacher asks her students to think about, add to, or revise two contracts she asked them to make with themselves:

- I will be the student I need to be in order to become the person I ought to be.
- I will practice the Platinum Rule. (The Golden Rule asks that we treat others the way we'd like to be treated; the Platinum Rule asks that we treat others the way they'd like to be treated.)

A 4th grade class crafts a set of agreements to live by. The teacher writes them on a poster and makes them available for several days so students can review them. Ultimately, each student who agrees to abide by the rules signs the poster—along with the teacher—and it is hung in the classroom so everyone can see it and refer to it for the remainder of the year.

- We agree to give *respect* to people, feelings, space, property, and ideas.
- We agree to be *responsible* for our actions, words, and choices.
- We agree to show *appreciation* for others and be inclusive and friendly.
- We agree to be *X-factor learners* and positive role models—modeling excellence, can-do attitudes, and our personal best!

A high school teacher uses three rules or guidelines with her students. They are terse and point to a way of life in the classroom that is enriching and empowering for all students.

- Take care of yourself.
- Take care of each other.
- Take care of this place.

Carrie Rothstein-Fisch and Elise Trumbull (2008) suggest the following straightforward and powerful rules or agreements:

- I am the best I can be.
- I follow directions the first time I hear them.
- I respect others as I wish to be respected.
- I am serious about learning.
- I am respectful.

When working with high school students who had generally lost trust in school and in their own ability to succeed in school and in life, high school history teacher Chad Prather (in Tomlinson, 2021) invited a respected community member to lead students in creating classroom guidelines they felt were respectful of them and supportive of their growth. The agreements they crafted together were spare but acknowledged the shared experiences of Chad's students, who had too often been subjected to rules imposed upon them. The process took a couple of class periods, but students participated honestly and, in the end, felt they had been heard and honored by the process. See pages 173–174 for more detail.

Rather than sounding distrustful of students or overburdening them with long lists of dos and don'ts, all of the student-created classroom rules we've shared set a tone of high expectations. They establish what's necessary and move learning to the foreground. Sometimes, of course, students will test or violate the rules they helped to create. Even adults sometimes find it difficult to adhere to principles that ask much of them. Certainly, young people may find it challenging to do what they know they should do. In Chapter 7, we'll propose some additional ideas for responding to students who push back and challenge classroom rules.

The remainder of this chapter focuses on procedures and routines that are common in differentiated classrooms and prepare students for working in such an environment. To help students learn and enact these routines, teachers should be sure to lead students to frequently consider the importance of the routines in creating a classroom that is effective for everyone, the role that classroom rules or agreements play, and how to make the routines function as they should.

Routines for Starting the Day or the Class

Students in the elementary grades typically enter a classroom in the morning and remain there for much of the day. As students progress through the grades, they tend to move from classroom to classroom. Although these two patterns present different opportunities and challenges for teachers, an effective beginning to the day (or to the class period) will likely address two needs regardless of age or grade. First, the beginning of the day or class should establish an affective tone that supports teaching and learning. Second, it should focus the students on learning. Whether they enter an elementary or secondary classroom, students will be switching environments and need to focus their attention on the expectations inherent to the new environment. To help students begin the day or class in a way that supports learning, think about incorporating the following steps into your start-up routine.

Consider using assigned or "home base" seats. When students have a specific place to sit as class begins, it's far more efficient for the teacher to take attendance, have materials and supplies positioned efficiently, and return student work. Most elementary students do have assigned or home base seats, at least in part because they store their own materials where they sit. There is a greater debate among middle and high school teachers about whether to assign seats, with some feeling that older students should have the privilege of choosing where to sit or that it's more respectful of students to let them make that choice. Our sense is that, in a differentiated classroom, students will move often and need to understand that. Assigning seats should not be a control mechanism but rather a way to begin the day or class efficiently and predictably. This same efficiency and predictability also come into play at the end of the day or class, when students return to their seats. This makes it easier to be sure materials and supplies are returned to appropriate places and that desks are clean and clear. It also facilitates common closure to class when students have been working on differentiated assignments. In addition, using assigned seats as class begins and ends, and on days when whole-class instruction is central, allows the teacher to avoid some common classroom seating hazards such as students opting out of participation by sitting in the back of the room, students arranging themselves by race or culture, ending up with the "haves" in one part of the room and the "have nots" in another, or cliques or "clots" of best buddies sitting together while not yet having the maturity to focus on learning when compelling distractions are nearby.

Be sure students know start-up expectations. Is there a particular place students should put their backpacks? What norms will govern when, if at all, students may use their mobile phones? Is there a board or other space in the classroom or online that they should check as they enter the room to get directions for picking up materials, beginning a task, or reviewing yesterday's work? Is there a place students should turn in homework as they enter the room, or someone who will check in their homework? Will there be a "sponge task" that students should begin as they get seated? If so, how long will they have to do the task? What purpose will it serve (e.g., review, thinking ahead, warming up)? Should they turn it in or keep the work when they finish? If you formally begin class before they finish the task, will you draw on what they have done as you begin conversation with the class? Must students be in their seats before a tardy bell begins to ring or before announcements begin? Should their desks be cleared, or should books, tablets, or notebooks be on their desks and ready for the start of class? What will signal the formal start of class—the teacher's voice, a bell, announcements? How should students respond to this signal? When students are clear about all of these sorts of expectations, the importance of the work of the class is highlighted. Order and predictability also contribute to a sense of safety for many students.

Use a "checking in" routine. For young students, morning meeting is a time when they can share things that are important to them and reconnect with the group. For older learners, teachers should take a bit of time to share a story, compliment the class or individual students on an achievement, or elicit some input about the way the class is working—and invite students to do the same. Effective teaching and learning are as much social and human endeavors as they are cognitive processes. Investing time in building a growing web of human connections will yield significant dividends in terms of trust, understanding, appreciation, community, and motivation to learn.

Review work plans. Be sure students know what they need to do, what high-quality work will look like, when and how to help one another (and when not to do so), how to access materials and supplies, and what to do when they finish a task. After students are comfortable with classroom routines, only a quick review or reminder will be necessary, but it's better to orient students for success than to handle the inevitable glitches that arise if students aren't clear about expectations.

Routines for Ending the Day or the Class

Just like the beginning of the day or class, it's important to end with clarity, purpose, and connections. Predictable routines for closure continue to provide parameters for an orderly, flexible classroom. They are also a key component in developing a sense of community in a differentiated classroom. Think about the following ideas as you develop your own routines for ending the day or class.

Give students advance notice. If students are working in small groups, give them a three- to five-minute signal to conclude their work and return materials and supplies to the appropriate places. Consider assigning only one or two students in each group to return materials and supplies and turn in the group's work. These roles should be assigned by you or determined by the group before work begins. Make sure students understand the need to keep the space in which they have been working clean, clear, and organized so everything is ready for the next day or class.

Signal a return to home base. Give students a one-minute signal when it is time to begin moving back to their assigned seats. This may be achieved most efficiently by moving quietly among the groups to provide a verbal signal to conclude their work, return materials, make sure the workspace is ready for the next subject or class, and return to assigned seats. It can also be done with a quick flick of the light switch or with an electronic timer on a whiteboard. Students should understand that they are expected to be in their seats by the end of the time you have indicated. Make sure students also know whether they will need to get supplies ready to take home for an assignment or ensure a clear desk upon their return to home base.

Remember to save time for closure. It's important to leave enough time at the end of the day or class to give a quick formative assessment, review how procedures and routines worked, look ahead to tomorrow, or review homework assignments. Most classes or days should end with two elements that are particularly important. First, there should be a brief closure discussion in which you review and/or students share common learning for the day or class. This not only solidifies for students the intended outcomes of their work, but it also reminds them of the important reality that, even though students in a differentiated classroom may sometimes work in different ways, they all work toward common goals and shared understandings. Second, there should once again be time to recognize the humanity of those who share the classroom. You might simply say, "When I go home today, I'm looking forward to playing with my new puppy—once I clean up after him! What are some of you looking forward to?" Alternatively, you might say, "I felt good that each of you was able to make a dent in the assignments you were doing today. I think two things contributed to that. The first is that you're getting really good at listening to directions in a way that helps you get right into your work. The second is that you've gotten quite skilled at helping one another get unstuck when you have a problem. Tell me how you're feeling about those things." It doesn't take long to renew each student's awareness of their interest in and commitment to the other individuals in the class and to the group as a whole.

Be sure students recognize their dismissal signal. This signal should nearly always come from you, not a bell or announcement. Make every effort to be ready to dismiss students as soon as the bell sounds or the announcements are complete, but in the few instances where it's useful for students to stay in place for a moment or two longer in order for the class to end smoothly, the teacher needs to mark the end of the day or class.

Routines for Assigning Students to Groups

Teachers need to address two questions when they assign students to flexible groupings in a differentiated classroom. First, how will students know *whom* they are working with on a particular day and at a particular time? Second, how will groups and individuals know *where* to work in the classroom? The ideas below provide guidance as you think about procedures to indicate and clarify answers to these questions for students.

Create standing groups. *Standing groups* are a foundational configuration that might last for a week, a month, or a unit before their membership changes, resulting in groupings that become familiar to students in membership, purpose, and perhaps even location in the classroom.

Figure 5.1 (see p. 132) suggests some ways teachers can assign standing groups in elementary classrooms. The upper two quadrants of the figure focus on a strategy called "grouping by the clock," with the upper left quadrant illustrating possible group sizes and purposes the teacher might have in mind during planning. Note that the name of the group (e.g., "11:00") does not indicate the time of day it will meet. An "11:00 group" may meet at 2:15 on one day and at 9:00 on another. The time designation is simply the name of the group. The teacher moves the hands of a cardboard clock or a clock face projected on a flat surface to signal which of the groupings students will work with at a given point in a lesson.

The clock in the upper right quadrant of Figure 5.1 is an example of group assignments sheet students might keep with their materials so they can quickly remind themselves of their 11:00 partners (those in their mixed-readiness quad), for example. The two lower quadrants of Figure 5.1 illustrate two other graphic formats a teacher could use to create and share student groupings to make transitions to standing groups easy and smooth. Figure 5.2 (see p. 132) provides one example of standing groups in a middle school class. There are many possibilities.

Standing groups are typically an augmentation or extension of a second kind of instructional group—those with which a teacher works daily or almost daily on foundational skills. *Foundational skill groups,* too, should change quite frequently, with students coming and going based on formative assessment information. If foundational skill groups begins to seem permanent or even semipermanent to the teacher or students, the teacher should think carefully about why that's the case. Why are students not progressing more rapidly, or why are students who have specific strengths or challenges in an area not moving to groups that

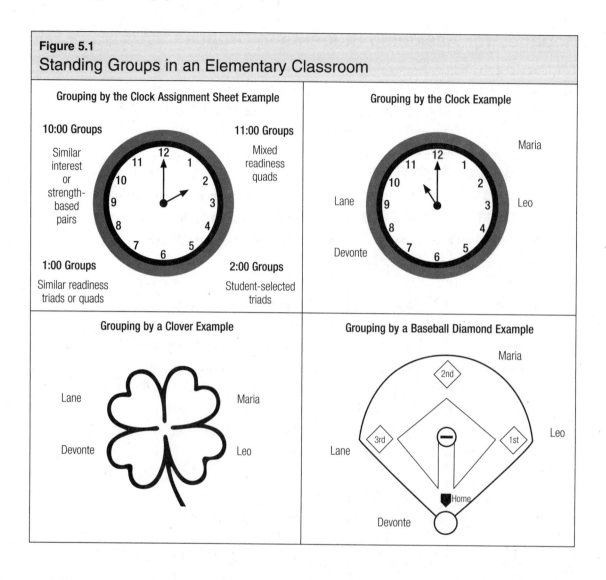

Figure 5.1
Standing Groups in an Elementary Classroom

Grouping by the Clock Assignment Sheet Example

10:00 Groups
Similar interest or strength-based pairs

11:00 Groups
Mixed readiness quads

1:00 Groups
Similar readiness triads or quads

2:00 Groups
Student-selected triads

Grouping by the Clock Example

Maria

Lane

Leo

Devonte

Grouping by a Clover Example

Lane

Maria

Devonte

Leo

Grouping by a Baseball Diamond Example

Maria

Lane

Leo

Devonte

Figure 5.2
Standing Groups in a Middle School Classroom

Text Teams	**Think Tanks**
Reading pairs composed of students with similar reading levels	Mixed-readiness writing idea generator groups of four or five
Synthesis Squads	**Samplers**
Groups of four with varied learning strengths (e.g., visual, performance, writing, metaphorical, analytical)	Groups of six with varied learning strengths and needs, used by the teacher to do quick "sampler" checks for progress and understanding
Teacher Talkers	**Peer Partners**
Groups of five to seven with similar learning needs and with whom the teacher will meet to extend and support growth	Student-selected groups of three or four used for a variety of purposes

are better suited to address those needs? Differentiation should never result in "tracking" or "ability grouping" within a classroom.

A third kind of instructional group that increases student engagement and understanding is the *spontaneous group*. For example, you may ask students to turn to their neighbors to summarize an idea, count off by sixes and then form groups of students with the same numbers, or work in triads to demonstrate what they understand about the science concept illustrated in a diagram, or to explain the main idea in a passage of prose or a model or a set of storyboards.

Code different areas of the room. When developing student groups (other than standing groups), create a system to designate or code areas of the room in a sort of shorthand that lets students readily know where they should move. This process allows you to attend to group composition and working location simultaneously. For example, a high school teacher refers to four quadrants of the room as the cardinal directions (north, south, east, and west). If the teacher says, "I'd like these students to meet in the south," everyone knows instantly what that means. Sometimes, the teacher uses additional regions such as northwest or southeast, but once students understand the layout, they can move quickly to the correct area. Other teachers might label table areas with numbers. For example, a round table in the corner is "Area 1," a nest of tables by the window is "Area 2," and so on. Another option is to project a floor plan or seating chart on a screen or wall with students' names written in the places where they should work on the upcoming task. The teacher simply says, "Please find your name on the chart and move quickly and quietly to the place where you'll be working today." Some names might appear in pairs, some in triads, some in quads, and some alone. The teacher might then say, "Find your name and the names of people you'll work with today if you're going to be part of a group. When I ask you to move, those of you who will be working independently, please go to the desks in the independent study area of the room. Those who will be working in pairs, please go to the front right corner of the room. Those working in groups of three should go to the front left corner of the room. Groups of four will be working in the back half of the room." Regardless of how you "code" the room, the goal is to give students a quick and clear indicator of where they will move for a particular task and whom, if anyone, they'll be working with.

Use pocket charts or assignment boards. Teachers of younger students often use pocket charts to let students know which tasks they'll be working on at a given time and who else may be working with them on the task (see Figure 5.3, p. 134).

Figure 5.3
Pocket Charts for Elementary School Classrooms

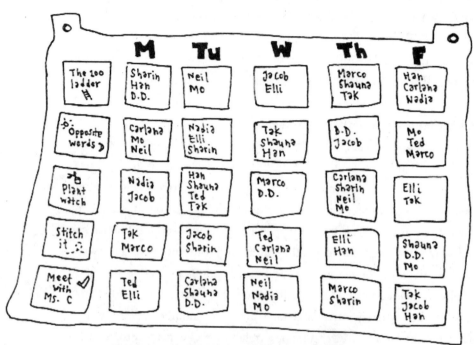

Teachers of older students can use assignment boards for the same purpose (see Figure 5.4). In both cases, students learn early in the year that certain activities are always located in the same areas of the room—for example, they go to a long table by the chalkboard when it's their turn to meet with the teacher, sit on the carpet in the front of the room to work with math flash cards, or go to the independent study area when they revise their writing. Pocket charts, task boards, and similar mechanisms for designating tasks and groups allow tremendous flexibility in groups and assignments targeted to the needs of members of a particular group. They also allow for control over the duration of both groupings and assignments while minimizing the amount of time necessary to organize students.

Figure 5.4
Assignment Board for Secondary School Classrooms

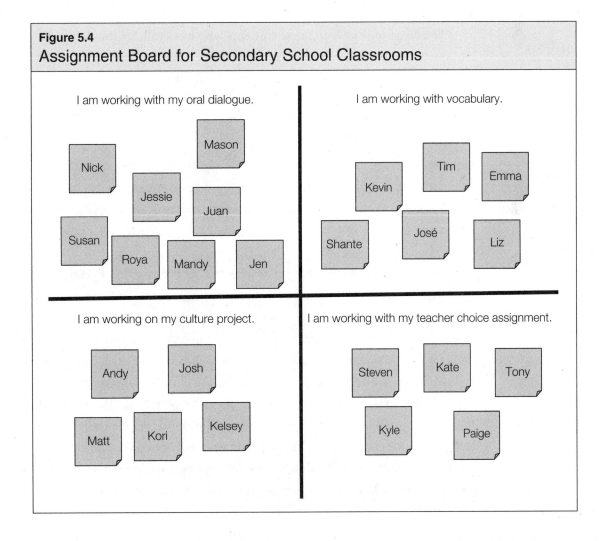

Routines for Giving Directions for Multiple Tasks

In a differentiated classroom, it is often the case that students will work on varied versions of the same task or even on different tasks during the same segment of time. Once students know who their working partners will be (if any) and where they should work in the classroom, they will then need clear directions for their assignment. There are many ways to be sure students know what to do as they begin working. The purpose of giving directions is, of course, student clarity about what to do and how to do it as efficiently as possible. Keeping these goals in mind can help the teacher decide which approaches make sense and which are likely to be counterproductive. Here are some suggestions for giving directions when students will work on varied tasks, versions of the same task, or in varied grouping arrangements.

Give directions only to those students who need to hear them. It generally creates confusion and wastes time if you give oral directions to the whole class for several tasks or versions of tasks. Inevitably, students hear directions other than their own, or they pay attention to whose work seems "better" than theirs. There may be some occasions when it seems important to explain to the whole class how or why varied tasks are alike and different. This is sometimes reassuring to students. For example, you may explain that today, some students will use books as a resource and others will use the computer, but tomorrow, they'll switch, and students who used the books today will use online resources tomorrow. Typically, however, it's not helpful to go over directions for tasks that certain students will not do.

Use task cards. Task cards are an effective means of giving directions to individuals or groups with varied work. In these instances, you might say, "When you move to the area of the room where you'll be working, you'll find a task card that will tell you what you need to do." Depending on the age and needs of the group, it may be wise to designate one student to read the task card to the group and then have one or two students summarize the directions before they move ahead. Task cards should clearly describe the task's goals (e.g., "As a result of this work, you should be able to…"), the steps involved, the materials needed to complete the task, and what high-quality work will look like. The latter can be addressed through class rubrics, work samples, or a statement that provides indicators of quality such as "Your work must show that you can use fractions to solve a measurement problem. It must also show that you can accurately explain how you arrived at your solution."

Provide directions in alternative formats. Recorded directions are particularly useful for young students, students who have difficulty reading, students who have difficulty following multistep oral directions, students learning English, or tasks that are multifaceted and complex. Small recording devices in appropriate settings allow students to hear directions, listen to directions given in a couple of ways, or replay directions as needed while they move through their work. For students who have difficulty completing multistep tasks, recorded directions might explain each step in a task and conclude each explanation with, "Do this step now. Check it with your teacher when you finish. When the teacher says you're ready for the next step, turn on the recording again and listen to the next part of the directions. Now turn off the recording." Alternatively, of course, you can use an intranet site to share videos that explain the assignment, provide criteria for success, or even review background information. Making this kind of information available on video means students who need additional or expanded opportunities to understand an assignment can access those opportunities readily and repeatedly. The caveat is that all students must have access to a computer and the internet. Assuming that access exists when, in fact, it does not further disadvantages students who already bring numerous limiting burdens to school with them daily.

Ask students to give directions. In every class, there are students who are good listeners, who remember what they hear, and who explain well to others. You can give directions to such students early in a class or the day before. When it's time for the larger group to work on the assignment(s), say, "When you get to the place in the room where you'll be working, someone in your group will give you directions."

Meet with students who have difficulty understanding directions. Students can have difficulty because they are learning English, because they have attention or reading disorders, because they find it confusing to follow multipart directions, or because they need to be close to the teacher to stay focused. Say, "I'd like to meet very briefly with the students whose names I'm going call out. You'll be joining your groups in just a minute or two." Then give directions to these students, have them paraphrase or summarize the directions, and ask them to say what steps they'll follow as they work. Students can then join their groups (or work independently) and be much more successful because they have increased clarity about what they need to do.

Differentiate the assignment. It's also possible, of course, to assign different tasks to students or ask them to pick up the correct assignment from a designated place in the room. For example, say, "The list of names on the board is in alphabetical order. Please find your name and notice the color that underlines your name. As you move to your work area for today, please pick up an assignment sheet that matches this color. For example, if your name is underlined in blue, pick up a blue assignment sheet. There are stacks of assignment sheets on the table in the front of the room and also on the bookshelves in the back of the room so we can avoid a traffic jam." Likewise, it works well to designate one student from the blue group to pick up five copies of the appropriate assignment to take back to the group. Again, when students have computer and internet access, you can give them links that will lead them to specifics about their particular assignment as well as links to resources that align with their reading proficiency, language needs, or preferred mode of accessing information (for example, a student with limited vision or a student with a specific reading disorder might do better accessing information via a podcast rather than a print article). A high school English teacher in a detracked honors class regularly directs all of her students to a website that contains common directions, goals, timelines, criteria for quality work, and in-common questions and resources for longer-term assignments. She also directs students to differentiated links, where they will find supports and additional resources targeted for their needs, strengths, and interests.

As students become competent and confident with these routines, they become increasingly aware of the role they play in their own learning, and they develop increasing ownership in the successful operation of the entire classroom. Chapter 6 will introduce additional routines that facilitate student and teacher success in a differentiated classroom. These routines are ones that are particularly valuable as students work in a flexible classroom setting.

6

Routines in a Differentiated Classroom
Once the Work Begins

[We saw beginning teachers in urban settings who] had a deep understanding of how children learn and how to structure tasks so that students could successfully undertake challenging intellectual work. They knew how to develop lessons that would add up to a curriculum that could achieve central academic goals, and they knew how to use assessments that would give them diagnostic information about each child so they could target students' individual needs. They built well-functioning communities among the students and a sense of responsibility for each other's welfare.

—Linda Darling-Hammond, *The Flat World and Education*

"Classroom environment" describes how a learning space looks, feels, and functions. It's an underrated factor in student success.

As she discusses urban settings in which teachers often have fixed mindsets about students; use scripted, low-level, and mechanized curricula; and aspire to run tight-ship classrooms, Linda Darling-Hammond (2009) points out that Maria, a young teacher in such an environment, and other teachers like her were able to see beyond stereotypes and low expectations to teach a complex curriculum that typifies the work of much older students in much more affluent settings. Darling-Hammond explains how this was possible:

> Maria created an environment in which each of her students was respected and enabled to participate actively and effectively. She avoided needing to chastise students by anticipating what normal busy children are likely to do and having a plan to keep them focused, well-behaved, and engaged in learning. Her careful planning allowed students to succeed at a complex task without punishment, discouragement, conflict, or failure. (p. 213)

This observation highlights several factors that are at work in learner-centered, responsive, or differentiated classrooms regardless of school context. First and most significantly, Maria did not subscribe to often-prevailing narratives about students who don't care about school and are persistently disruptive in class. Instead, she respected the capacity of each learner to do complex, collaborative, and relevant work. She translated this conviction into lessons that signaled to her students her belief in them and her high expectations of them. In other words, she envisioned "classroom management" as an orchestration of rich, meaningful learning opportunities—not a tool for controlling student behavior. The care Maria took to plan engaging work for her students and to develop with her students routines that both supported their success and minimized catalysts for commotion, frustration, and counterproductive behavior was key to providing equitable access to excellent learning opportunities for the full range of students in her classroom.

This is the power of mindfully and proactively planning details in the classroom. Paradoxically, teachers who give meticulous care to establishing routines ultimately *free* their students to work. The routines spotlighted in this chapter are enacted as the work of a differentiated class is enacted. The routines anticipate what might go wrong in a room full of students and are designed to prevent those problems from arising. In the end, routines should make teaching and learning more effective and efficient because they support both endeavors. The routines and procedures that follow are primarily for students, but some are for teachers. For all of them, however, it's important that both students and teachers understand the goals of a differentiated classroom and how a particular routine or procedure helps achieve those goals.

Routines for Calling on Students

It's remarkably easy for teachers to get into the habit of calling on students who volunteer to answer questions and allowing those who are shy, detached, or lacking in confidence to opt out of active participation in classroom discourse. This practice allows mental dropouts to evolve, and it no doubt contributes to physically dropping out as well. In a differentiated classroom, the value placed on the success of each student necessitates practices that are inclusive and engage each learner. One teacher signals this idea to her students by saying, "In here, nobody gets to be invisible."

There are two key goals to developing routines for calling on students:

- Make sure everyone in the class has both the opportunity and responsibility to speak.
- Develop a system that helps students make meaningful contributions to class discussions, conversations, or deliberations.

A high school history teacher explains to her students that she feels her role in discussions is to prepare intriguing and important questions for the class to consider. "Your role," she says to her students, "is to be prepared to share your perspectives on the questions. Every one of you has something valuable to contribute to our thinking. I will call on you in ways that ensure each of you has a voice here." She uses three methods to call on students during whole-class discussions. In "Bag of Names," she writes the names of all her students on small slips of paper and collects them in a small lunch bag. She draws names from the bag and calls students randomly. She also uses a "Volunteers" approach in which she encourages students who want to make a contribution or a point to do so—an important time for students with advanced knowledge, strong opinions, or an itch to be heard. Finally, she calls for "New Voices"—students who have not spoken during Bag of Names or Volunteers. She reminds students of their responsibility to share their perspectives with the class, and students respond appropriately.

To ensure that all students participate—including those who are learning the language of the classroom, those who have not seen themselves (and who have not been seen) as smart, those who are reticent, and those who feel unprepared because of a lack of background experience—the teacher uses a variety of approaches that students come to understand and appreciate. Sometimes, she might prime a student for a question by saying, "In a minute, Josh, I'm going to ask your opinion about the benefits of the amendment for the development of the United States, but first, I want to hear from one more person about why it may have taken so long for the amendment to pass." She then calls on someone from the bag of names for the latter question, giving Josh, who responds more confidently with some thinking time, the opportunity to mentally prepare an answer for the question the teacher will ask him.

At another point, she calls on a student who does not know an answer or who does not have the vocabulary to express it. Seeing the student's hesitancy, she says, "Give me a word or phrase that comes to your mind when you think about the question." She then draws another name from the bag and says, "Please build on Annanji's idea." The second student then expands on the initial idea, and the teacher repeats this process with another student or two before returning to Annanji to say, "Let me repeat the question now, Annanji, and you tell us what you think is important to consider as we try to answer it." Inevitably, the hesitant student can provide an expanded response. Students become accustomed to building on one another's ideas and sometimes say, "I'll say what I'm thinking now, but maybe some other people in the class could build on my idea." Figure 6.1 provides some additional ways to call on students to ensure that everyone in the class has both the opportunity and responsibility to be a contributor to class discussions.

Remember, however, that for some students, the fear of being called on in class can trigger significant anxiety. These students may have speech disorders, be extremely shy, be victims of bullying, or carry emotional burdens that make it difficult for them to get through a school day. Whatever the cause of their fears, teachers should take care not to add to the discomfort they feel. The burden already makes it difficult, if not impossible, for the brain to attend to learning (Sousa & Tomlinson, 2018). Be sure to demonstrate understanding and empathy for these students' feelings and stress to them that you value their ideas and want to find a way to hear from them without calling on them in class. Then work with them to find that way.

Consider, for example, privately saying to the student that you have observed their discomfort with speaking in class and ask if your observation is accurate. Tell the student that you will certainly honor their preference not to speak in class unless the student raises a hand or tells you at some point in the future that it is OK to call on them. Tell the student that you still want to hear their ideas about discussions in some way and suggest possibilities such as the student keeping a journal of ideas and questions that occur to them during discussions and submitting it every few days, responding to discussions via daily or weekly emails to you, or recording thoughts and questions briefly in the evening after a discussion and emailing them to you as voice memos. Clarify for the student how you'll respond—perhaps briefly on most days, or every three or four days, or once a week. Invite the student to share other ideas about ways to help you "hear" their voice.

Figure 6.1
Methods to Call on Students Equitably

Strategy	Explanation
Name Sticks	For younger students, draw student names (written on tongue depressors or craft sticks) from a cup to have them answer questions or share ideas in the classroom. Ask the question(s) first so that all students must think of a response before they know who will be asked to answer. When a question has a student stumped, they are allowed to ask for help from a classmate.
Spinner System	Use a system of assigning students to table groups (usually with four students to a group), classify the groups by color, and give each group member a number. Use spinners to determine the color and number for a variety of tasks. For example, student 3 from the orange group might be asked to respond. If spinners are not available as part of your instructional tools, homemade versions are easy to construct. They are also readily available in children's board games and in online versions.
Baseball Cards	Ask students from upper elementary and middle school classrooms to create a baseball card that has their picture on the front (these can be school pictures or photos taken in class) and "statistics" that reveal something about the student (e.g., family information, hobbies, goals) on the back. Use the cards to learn more about each student and to randomly call on students to respond. This can be done in a variety of exciting ways, such as how a professional card player would draw a card.
Computer-Generated Names	A random, computer-generated list of student names is quite easy to use and motivating for students. This can be used at any grade level, but it is especially helpful for secondary teachers who often teach many students and for whom computer-generated lists can be a time-saver.

Routines for Working in Groups

As anyone who has ever watched school boards, city councils, state or national legislatures, or teacher committees in action can tell you, working in groups is complicated. On many levels, it's easier to be a soloist than a member of an ensemble. Nevertheless, most experts tell us that collaboration and the use of collective intelligence to solve problems are skills our students must develop if they are to be prepared for life in the world beyond school (e.g., Brookhart & Rasooli,

2021; Cohen & Lotan, 2014; Fullan et al., 2018; Zhao, 2009, 2022). Students can learn to work effectively in groups in the same ways that they learn mathematical operations, the skills of a sport, or proficiency in singing—with instruction, guidance, and practice. In other words, teachers need to teach students how to work in groups effectively. They also need to establish opportunities for students to work together in meaningful and productive ways on assignments that are important and engaging. It's in this context that students can develop and polish their skills of collaboration.

As you develop procedures, guidelines, and routines for group work, and as you design the work groups will do, consider (and make sure your students understand) the following skills for effective group work:

- Being prepared for the work of the group by completing preparatory assignments and by entering the group with the intent to contribute to its success.
- Understanding the parameters of the work, including its goals, success criteria, timelines, and possible resources to support understanding.
- Making a plan to accomplish the work of the group, including creating an effective division of labor that matches individual strengths with key goals.
- Evaluating the group's progress toward achieving goals throughout the span of the group work and adjusting plans as needed to ensure quality work.
- Listening to one another carefully.
- Speaking to one another respectfully.
- Asking questions that clarify goals, understandings, and processes for all members of the group.
- Working together as supportive members of a team.
- Understanding that mistakes not only are inevitable but also can be a source of important learning.
- Being empathetic when group members have difficulty.
- Helping one another solve problems.
- Making and responding to suggestions.

Design group tasks that support both meaningful collaboration and student achievement of desired outcomes. You want to make sure that

- Students understand the task goals.
- The task tightly aligns with learning goals (i.e., it leads students directly to what they should know, understand, and be able to do).

- Most students will find the task interesting.
- Students understand what's expected of them as individuals in support of the group's work.
- Students have access to materials that are a match for their language proficiencies and that offer varied media or formats to support understanding of a wide range of learners.
- The task requires genuine collaboration in order to achieve shared understanding (i.e., it cannot be done more effectively by an individual or subset of students in the group than by the group as a whole).
- The task requires an important contribution from each group member by drawing on the strengths of the individuals in the group.
- The task is challenging for the group and its members.
- The pace of the work is brisk (but not rigid), and students feel the need to remain focused on the work.
- The group is responsible for a shared understanding of the content of the work and group processes.
- There are opportunities for teacher or peer coaching during the task.
- The task incorporates in-process quality checks that will support productive use of student time and strong outcomes.
- Students understand what to do after they complete their work at a high level of quality.

Two early researchers in the dynamics of effective group work, Elizabeth Cohen and Rachel Lotan (2014), commend group work that uses heterogeneous groups in terms of both current student achievement and areas of strength in which students collaborate to solve complex, open-ended, and uncertain problems built around concepts and principles of a discipline. Such work provides a path to equity of opportunity for a very broad range of students to access excellent learning opportunities and to learn the skills of productive collaboration. In that context, Cohen and Lotan describe what they call "groupworthy tasks" (p. 85) with the following hallmarks:

- They are open-ended, uncertain in ways that challenge students to do productive thinking, and require complex problem solving.
- They provide opportunities to use multiple strengths and intellectual abilities to access the tasks and to demonstrate intellectual competence.
- They address discipline-based, intellectually important content.

- They require positive interdependence among group members as well as individual accountability.
- They include clear criteria for evaluating both the group's product and the individual's report. (p. 85)

More recently, Michael Toth and David Sousa (2019), whose work in both psychology and neuroscience has expanded our understanding of teaching and learning, have advocated using a process called student-led academic teaming to prepare students to be responsible for the learning of their team members and to not only learn academic content but also grow in decision making, social and emotional skills, appreciation of cultural diversity, and sustaining attention. As is the case with the Cohen and Lotan model, the Toth and Sousa model incorporates productive struggle, individual accountability, and group interdependence. While the intent of group work generally is to involve every student in a class in effectively guided collaboration with peers, there are sometimes students who, for a variety of reasons, cannot meaningfully contribute to or benefit from group collaboration. Perhaps they have ongoing struggles with paying attention, social skills, or emotional volatility. Perhaps they are hindered by the challenge of learning and communicating in a language that is new to them. Perhaps they are just having a bad day. Arranging groups so that students who are struggling with collaboration challenges can work alongside students who are willing and able to serve as mentors can be bridge to success. Of course, it is important for the teacher to coach the mentor student in understanding the kinds of help that might be useful for the mentee in specific assignments and in general—and for the teacher to be attuned to both successes and ongoing needs of the mentor student and the student receiving support.

When a student cannot succeed in a group at a particular time because of restlessness, behaviors that negatively impact the work of the group, or emotional challenges, it is wise for a teacher to provide a "way out" for that student so that neither the student who is struggling nor the other students have to suffer. If mentor students and other group members work responsibly to support one another, and a struggling student continues to have or create difficulty working in the group, talk with that student privately and ask them to work independently (in a predetermined quiet zone in the room) on a meaningful task for the remainder of the group work time. This should not be done punitively or with anger; simply explain that working with the group is not productive at the moment, and an alternative seems like a better idea. Later, talk with the student again to see if they can identify the cause of friction with the group, and determine some ways to address the issue. Work with the student to help them reenter the group successfully when the time is right. This may mean talking with the group about its processes, closely monitoring the group to suggest adjustments, or making it possible for the student to work with the group for shorter periods of time (long enough to experience success with the group but not so long that problems arise). Some students who grapple with emotional disorders, trauma, or other major disruptors to learning may need to work independently while teachers and specialists continue to work with them to understand and manage their counterproductive behaviors (Tomlinson, 2022).

If necessary, it's fine to say to the class (which, no doubt, is keenly aware of any problems one of its members may have with group or individual interactions), "You know, some of us find it very challenging to spell words correctly. Some of us have a hard time writing. Some of us find it really tough to memorize things. Some of us find it difficult to work in group settings. That's OK, because we all have the ability to get better at the things we find to be difficult. I'll ask you to work hard on the things that are difficult for you, and I hope you'll try to help one another with challenges as well. I'm confident every one of us can succeed with challenging things."

Routines for Managing Noise

It's important for students to talk with one another at appropriate times in order to learn together. It's also easy for conversations among students (even those who are completely focused on their work) to escalate, simply because 25 to 40 voices in a relatively small space can be overwhelming. The goal in an orderly, flexible classroom is not "no noise" but rather "productive noise." Making noise work in favor of learning—rather than against it—is a maintenance issue in classes where students work collaboratively. However, it need not be a problem so much as a detail to which the teacher and students attend, such as keeping pencils sharpened or making sure materials are straight and stored properly.

Think about the following ideas as you develop routines for handling noise in the classroom.

Clarify student expectations. Be sure students understand that you want them to work with you to monitor their conversations. This helps them work together effectively and successfully.

Place a value on silent work. Teach students what it means to work silently, and enforce this rule by routinely asking them to do so for specific, generally limited, periods of time. It's helpful to introduce activities that require silence very early in the year so students develop a point of comparison and know how to transition to silence when needed. If the whole class struggles to maintain silence, ask students to work silently for brief periods that are slightly shorter than the length of time they can remain silent. This ensures success from the outset. You can then gradually extend the lengths of silent work expected of them.

A vibrant class includes the sounds of students talking together, being excited about their work, and finding joy in the work they do. Silence is not the predominant feature of an effectively differentiated classroom. However, it can be a useful element in supporting students who need quiet, providing periods of calm that enable students to recalibrate, supporting student focus on complex tasks, and doing person-specific work students need to take their next steps in learning.

Define acceptable noise limits. Develop indicators of or terms for various noise levels that you and the students can use with mutual understanding. Then translate them into a routine that establishes and monitors classroom noise. Consider the following examples.

Remind young students to reduce their voice levels by saying, "Scholars, give me five." Students then stop what they were doing, open their hands, and bend their fingers toward their palms as you count down from five—pinkie first, ring finger second, middle finger third, and thumb fourth. With their index fingers extended, say "one" as students put their fingers in front of their closed lips. The few seconds of silence, along with the established quiet signal, remind students to begin working again very quietly. Alternatively, you might say, "Folks, VW." Students stop their conversations and follow suit as you alternately hold up two and three fingers, switching between a *V* and a *W*. The students should understand that "VW" means "voices, whisper." Again, the reminder has the desired effect.

In an elementary classroom, you might post a construction-paper stoplight. Green represents noise at a conversational level, yellow is a whisper, and red is complete silence. An arrow beside the appropriate level for a particular task helps students get ready to transition into a new task. If the noise rises above the appropriate level, say, "Eyes up front, everyone. Stoplight check." Likewise, a "noiseometer," made to look like a thermometer, can also indicate noise levels from "acceptable" to "uncomfortable" to "unacceptable."

When voices rise beyond a comfortable level, say (in a slightly raised voice), "If you can hear me, clap once." A few students will likely respond, but the sound of their clapping will get the attention of others. In a softer voice, say, "If you can hear me, clap twice." Continue this pattern, increasing the number of claps and reducing voice volume, until the count of four or five. (By two or three, most students will be listening and clapping along.) After five claps, remind students to monitor their conversation level to be sure it's not distracting to others.

Delineate four categories of voice levels: "mute button" (i.e., no sound), "six-inch voices" (i.e., someone standing or sitting more than six inches away from you cannot hear what you are saying), "work voices" (i.e., appropriate, conversational levels), and "playground/hall voices" (i.e., unacceptably loud levels for the classroom). Students should learn to shift to "six-inch voices" or to push the "mute button" when reminded to do so.

Designate one student in each group whose role is to monitor the voice level of the group. Remind students of appropriate voice levels as you walk around the classroom, and compliment groups when they talk at the designated level.

Allow students to block out distracting noise and visual overload. Sometimes, there are students in a class who are very sensitive to noise and are distracted even when classmates are talking at acceptable levels. It can be beneficial for those students to use headsets with "cuffs" that sit around the ears and help mute noise. Inexpensive earplugs (available in drugstores, airports, and online) can also help students who need to reduce or eliminate surrounding noise. In the latter instance, keep sets of assigned earplugs in a designated place in the room. For students who are distracted by visual "noise," consider using portable carrels made of heavy cardboard that can be easily set up and stored. It may also be possible to have some desks facing away from bulletin boards and other visual stimuli that are troubling for some learners.

Routines for Getting Help

Students often learn to see the teacher as their primary, if not exclusive, source of help in the classroom when they work independently or in small groups. Although teachers will always need to be key players in a classroom support system, when they are the predominant source of help, there's no time to teach individual students or small groups of students, no time to conduct systematic observations of students, no time to observe patterns in the work habits of individuals or groups. As a result, the teacher performs functions that someone else could handle and gives up roles only the teacher can play. However, when students learn routines for getting help while they work independently and in small groups, the teacher is free to do targeted teaching and strategic observation. Consider the following ideas.

Develop clear directions. Invest time in developing directions—written, oral, or both—that you will ask students to follow. They should be brief, use accessible vocabulary, proceed in a step-by-step manner, and not skip any steps. To avoid as much confusion as possible, formulate your direction to anticipate ways in which students might misinterpret them. For students who struggle with reading, using icons and recordings as substitutes for or additions to written directions can be quite helpful.

Teach students to be active listeners. Make a game out of seeing who can summarize directions or repeat the last thing you said. As they become conscious listeners, students are better able to help themselves proceed with a task. Many questions come from students who don't listen well in the first place, because they know you will repeat the directions if they didn't hear them the first time.

Make sure students know when to ask you for help. Teach students when it's all right to come to you for help and when it's not. (An emergency is always the right time for a student to come to you!) In a differentiated classroom, there will be times when the teacher is off-limits, such as when you are working with individuals or small groups or when students are making transitions from one task or position to another. In the former instance, it's important to have uninterrupted time to work with individuals and small groups. In the latter instance, it's useful to be unencumbered to monitor student movement around the room and to make sure students settle into their new workspaces smoothly. In general, it contributes to "clutter" in the classroom if students can get up and approach you at any time for questions, for supplies, or to turn in papers. For this reason, alternative routines for getting help are valuable.

Make sure students know when and how to ask their peers for help. In general, classmates are excellent sources of help, and when students learn to pull together and help one another, both collegiality and community develop. When there is a reason for students not to ask peers—or certain peers—for help because of the nature of an assignment or because a student has requested not to provide help, be sure the class is aware of who or what is off-limits.

Use "question chips." Give each student one or two poker chips, or other small plastic disks, at the beginning of the day. When they ask *you* for help, they must pay one chip (questions to classmates are "free"). Once their chips are gone, they have no choice but to rely on their peers for help. It's important to not be too rigid with the chips. Continue to move among students as they work, asking if they need help (questions that you pose to students are also "free"). The goal is not to deprive students of the assistance they need but to expand the sources of help they feel comfortable drawing upon.

Administer "first aid." In elementary classrooms, it can be helpful to have a "first aid" area on the classroom wall. Beneath the area, students' names are printed on large pieces of cardboard made to look like bandages. Students who try to get assistance from two classmates but still need your help should post their bandages on the "first aid" board. Check the board often as you move from group to group so you know who needs help quickly. Some teachers use green or red.

Figure 6.2 provides additional examples of routines to ensure that students get timely assistance.

Figure 6.2
Methods to Ensure Students Receive Help When Needed

Strategy	Explanation
Expert of the Day	One of many jobs students might have in a classroom is to play the role of "Expert of the Day." Students in this role are the designated "go to" person on a particular topic, assignment, or procedure. Every student knows that they will have a turn in this role, so they all understand they are capable of helping others. Teachers of young children sometimes use visors with "Ask Me" written on the bill. Teachers of older students generally designate Experts of the Day orally or on the board.
Colored Cups	Colored drinking cups are placed on student tables when groups are working together. Students use the cups to indicate the status of their work. A green cup on top of the stack means "Our group is working well and doesn't need help." A yellow cup means "We think we're OK, but we're not absolutely sure." A red cup means "We're stuck and can't go on." The cups indicate where immediate help is most important. It's also useful to note patterns in the cups. When groups never need help, it may mean the work is too easy for the group. When one group often has a red cup on top of the stack, it might be that the work is too difficult for them and more differentiation is necessary. This method can be adapted to signal individual students' need for help.
Question Cards	Question cards are an individual signal students use to indicate a need for assistance. Students fold a large index card in the middle and draw a large question mark on both sides of the card. They then stand the sign on their desk like a placard if they have used other sources of help but are still uncertain of how to move ahead with their work. The cards efficiently signal where help is needed.
Mini-Workshops	Mini-workshops are typically teacher initiated and result from observations made while moving around the room, such as noticing that several students have difficulty with the same skill or have a similar misunderstanding. You might say, "As I'm looking at your work, I see that several of you are a bit fuzzy on how to reduce a fraction. If you're not really confident of how to do that, meet with me on the floor in the front of the room." Students who need help benefit from a quick review and an opportunity to ask questions before returning to their work. You can also use mini-workshops to help individual students as necessary. It's possible for students to request a mini-workshop independently if they realize several of them are struggling with a particular skill or idea.

Routines for Transitioning Between Tasks and Workspaces

In a differentiated classroom, students regularly move among whole-class, small-group, and independent work. These shifts often include different student groupings, the need for different materials, and the necessity to move to various parts of the room. Although any student of any age is capable of making these transitions smoothly, they also have the capacity to generate a good deal of disruption and distraction as they move between tasks and places. The following suggestions should be useful as you plan routines for classroom transitions.

Clarify expectations. Discuss with students what will be necessary to enable a large number of them to move from place to place in the classroom, get supplies, and settle in to do work effectively. They should be able to identify elements such as walking quietly, moving quickly from place to place in the most direct way, limiting talking during transitions, paying attention to where they need to be and what they need to take with them (rather than being concerned about where classmates are going), and getting seated as soon as possible.

Create a time challenge. Time students as they shift locations early in the year. Challenge them to make transitions as quickly as they can without running or getting in one another's way. Students quickly learn that they are expected to move efficiently, and they retain that pattern throughout the year. Post the "best time" or a timer on the board to motivate students to make transitions quickly—and quietly.

Organize materials logically. Store materials and supplies in locations around the perimeter of the room so students can retrieve and return items with minimal movement through the center of the room (where peers are working). Students quickly learn to walk around the perimeter rather than across the room to get what they need.

Designate "supply couriers." When students will be using a common set of materials in a group, it is generally more efficient for one student to get the materials for the entire group during a transition or work time rather than have each student get the materials. This same student could be responsible for asking questions (at the appropriate time) or having work checked. This reduces the amount of traffic and potential chaos caused by multiple students from each group moving around the room or vying for your attention. Finally, it often makes sense for one student per group to return materials, supplies, and student folders as work ends and students transition again. Also consider assigning one or two students from the class to do a quick tour of the classroom to make sure that seating areas are clear and clean and that all materials and supplies are in the right places at the end of transitions.

Post alternative seating plans. Create multiple room arrangement charts and post them on a bulletin board. For example, they might be labeled "Discussion Format," "Current Events Format," "Seminar Format," and "Team Format." All charts should include all of the room's furniture in varied arrangements. With guidance, students practice moving the furniture into the different arrangements several times (quickly and quietly), and they learn where to move their home base seats to accommodate each of the arrangements. Within a very short time, students will be able to change the entire room configuration with precision and speed. This provides tremendous flexibility in using classroom space, and students become proud of their "drill team" moves.

Routines for Managing Time

It's never the case in any classroom that students all finish an assignment at exactly the same moment—or that all students need exactly the same amount of time to achieve mastery in a particular area. A differentiated classroom differs from others in that it recognizes and accommodates "ragged time." Such accommodations exist on two levels—one focuses on the need for flexibility in the short term, the other in the longer term. In the short term, *student* routines are needed for what students should do when they complete a task before the teacher "calls time" or when a student needs a bit more time to complete an assignment. In the longer term, the *teacher* must have routines that allow forward and backward teaching at the same time. Think about the following strategies as you develop student and teacher routines for managing time.

Plan instructional time in terms of "highways and exit ramps." "Highway time" is largely whole-class time and should focus all students on the essential knowledge, understanding, and skills that are core to a unit or inquiry. It includes elements like minilessons or minilectures, reading (often differentiated for access by all students) followed by whole-class or small-group conversations, small-group processing and applying ideas and skills, watching or participating in demonstrations related to the essential learning targets, planning for upcoming products or performances, and other instructional elements that make learning active, collaborative, and compelling. "Exit ramp time" includes working in small groups with the teacher, practicing student's next steps in terms of skills or knowledge mastery, or pursuing their own interests (perhaps related to current content or perhaps as an opportunity to apply foundational skills such as reading, writing, research, planning, evaluating, and so on). Exit ramp time enables each learner to regularly take their own next steps in growth in dimensions of learning that are pivotal for that student. Consistent use of both highways and exit ramps in instructional planning enables all learners to work with compelling content that opens the way to learning success in the classroom and beyond while actively supporting each learner in what John Hattie (2012) calls "plus-one learning," noting that teachers should "plan for each learner to move forward every day at least one step (one chunk, one skill, one idea, one insight…) beyond a student's entry point on that day" (Tomlinson, 2022, p. 143).

Introduce anchor activities very early in the year. An anchor activity is a task (or a set of tasks) to which students move when they complete an assignment. Figure 6.3 lists characteristics of quality anchor activities. Create a routine for moving from an assignment to an anchor activity. Should students check the quality of their completed assignment with you? With a peer? Where should the completed work go? Where are anchor options located in the room? May any student choose any anchor task? Do students sit where they were previously seated to work on the anchor activity? How should they work with the anchor task so that they are not distracting peers? Is there any time limit or expectation with any of the anchor options? Is there a procedure for getting help with an anchor task? What should they do with completed work when the teacher needs to see the work—turn it in, put it in a work folder, or something else?

Figure 6.3
Characteristics of High-Quality Anchor Activities

❒ Activities are focused on essential learning goals (not tangential or trivial).
❒ Activities are engaging (not rote practice).
❒ Activities address a broad range of student interests and help make content relevant for students from a variety of backgrounds.
❒ Activities address a broad range of readiness needs and vary from concrete to abstract, structured to open-ended, and simple to complex.
❒ Activities allow for a variety of ways of taking in and expressing ideas that address a broad range of learning profile needs.
❒ Activities are presented with clear directions so students know what to do, what the final product should be, how they will know when they are finished, and what to do with the work they generate.
❒ Activities incorporate a monitoring system so the teacher and students can recognize the level of quality produced and any need for adjustment.

Add to the list of anchor options gradually. Start the year with a small set of anchor activity options and add new ones as students become familiar with them and as the curriculum expands. Students will be able to suggest or create their own anchor activities as the year progresses.

Do not grade anchor activities. Look at the work students are doing to provide brief feedback and encouragement. The clear and persistently reinforced ethic of a differentiated classroom simply needs to be "there are so many interesting things to learn, it's never acceptable to just stop working." When finished with an assignment, a student should automatically start an anchor activity as the *next* assignment. All students should understand that you've designed anchor activities to be interesting, be accessible, and increase their sense of competence. Invite students to suggest their own ideas for anchor activities. You may want to give students a "mark" (not a grade) for how well they work with these tasks as a mechanism for discussing their work habits and habits of mind.

Explain the ground rules for extra time. Determine and share with students conditions under which it's likely for them to get additional time to work on an assignment after you "call time" for the class on an assignment. For example, if you observe that a student worked very diligently on the task but simply needs a bit more time, it makes sense to provide that time. It may also be important to give a student extra time to work on a task if they seem eager to pursue the topic in greater depth. On the other hand, it may not be wise to give a student additional time to complete a piece of work if they wasted time or didn't focus on the task. Still, it's necessary to look beyond the surface. It may be that the student has enduring attention problems or that they didn't focus on the work because it was much too difficult or much too easy. You want to provide time for students to finish the work if it seems beneficial to do so without fostering a sense that if they lollygag, they'll get a reprieve. On extended assignments, such as projects or performance assessments, a "petition for extended time" may be useful with older learners. The petition should make the case for an extension, and this process tends to signal to students the difference between *needing* more time to achieve high-quality work and *wanting* more time because of procrastination. Figure 6.4 (see p. 156) provides an example of a petition created for secondary students.

Teachers in differentiated classrooms need their own routines for handling the inevitability that some students will be ready to move ahead in content before others, that some students will need to linger on a topic in order to develop key competencies and understandings, and that some students will need to revisit content from earlier years to move ahead effectively with the current year's content goals. In other words, teachers in effectively differentiated classrooms learn to teach forward and backward at the same time. Consider the following strategies as you think about these scenarios.

Figure 6.4
Petition for an Extension of Time on a Project

Student's Name: _____

Date: _____

Project: _____

In the space below, please make your case for requesting an extension of time on this piece of work. Remember that extensions will only be granted in cases where (1) there is good evidence that you used your time on the project effectively, (2) you made sure the teacher was aware of your progress throughout the assignment period, and (3) there is solid evidence that extended time will allow you to develop a product of very high quality.

Length of the extension you are requesting: _____

Decision of the teacher: _____

Teacher comments:

Develop procedures for providing meaningful challenge for advanced learners. Figure 6.5 indicates some strategies teachers can use to challenge advanced learners who have mastered the content that most of the class still needs to study.

Figure 6.5
Methods to Challenge Advanced Learners

Strategy	Explanation
Complex Applications of Content	An advanced learner may be challenged by using current knowledge, understanding, and skills in applications that are unfamiliar, abstract, or multifaceted. Asking these students to use multiple sets of skills simultaneously to address problems that don't have a ready solution can also be challenging. For example, Trey's 3rd grade teacher worked with his school's resource teacher for advanced learners to find a real-world math problem for him to pursue. Trey had to use addition, subtraction, and multiplication, in addition to basic geometry, to solve the problem. Although he had studied those concepts in class, he seldom had to use multiple operations at once. Ultimately, Trey became excited about thinking his way through an approach to math that was new to him.
Advanced and Extended Resources	Challenge can result from a student's use of advanced resources such as books, websites, or contacts with experts to gain a deeper understanding of a topic. For example, employees at a local fish hatchery suggested some internet and print resources that 7th grader Luis could use to learn about endangered fish species in his area. Because Luis had an advanced level of knowledge about several topics in his science unit, his teacher encouraged him to develop a project examining potential ways to protect the species and to offer his solutions and suggestions to an environmental agency. The project lasted for several months, and Luis worked on it in lieu of two differentiated unit projects completed by most of his classmates.
Focus on Interest	Some students may be advanced in one content area but not be particularly intrigued by that area. In such instances, students can learn about an area of personal interest with time that they can "buy" because of early mastery of the required content. For example, Matt learned math very quickly in 5th grade and often needed much less time than his peers to master a topic. Although he didn't find math particularly interesting, he was very eager to learn about anthropology. Matt and his teacher developed a long-term anthropology investigation that he would work on when he finished a math unit early.
Making Connections	Students often study subjects in school in a disconnected way. Therefore, it can be exciting and challenging for them to discover connections across content areas. For example, Jana was a very strong reader and also knew a lot about social studies. Her teacher worked with her to develop an ongoing anchor activity for her in which she read novels and biographies about the time periods and people she and her classmates were studying in school. Jana kept a journal about connections she saw across her readings (in response to questions posed by her teacher and based on her own insights). She worked on the anchor activity when she mastered social studies content rapidly, when she finished any class task early, and when there was a social studies or language arts homework assignment her teacher felt she didn't need to complete.
Moving On	Advanced learners sometimes have great talent in one content area and a hunger to learn more about it. In such instances, it may be that the only meaningful challenge is for students to move ahead at their own pace. This can be accomplished by providing appropriately leveled text materials and support with those materials. Sometimes, a learner may need to work with students in a more advanced grade level in a particular subject, and the school will need to work with the student and their parents to examine the pros and cons of advancing the student's grade level. The goal should be to find the best possible source of challenge for that student at a particular time. Results should be monitored carefully and modified if necessary.

With these strategies in place, students recognize that there is a consistent plan for their growth, and they don't develop expectations for "success" with little effort. Be sure you work *with* these students, as with all students, to provide them with important teacher connections, to support them when work seems too difficult to them (which should frequently be the case for these learners and seldom is in school), and to provide feedback on their work. Don't forget to make these students your partners in planning work that enriches and extends them as learners. Like all students, they need and deserve voice in their learning. They often have insights that might not occur to their teachers and that can benefit their growth—and ours as well.

Advanced students need teacher support and attention as much as any other student does—especially if their work is *truly* appropriately challenging. They also will likely need you to help them identify learning opportunities that are robust and meaningful and to move forward with that work. When possible, coplanning or coteaching with a specialist in gifted education can help you understand how to develop student work at an advanced level of challenge. Recall always that meaningful challenge does not stem from asking students to do more of what they have already mastered or from work that is "hard." "Hard work" is tedious and burdensome and feels punitive. Intellectually challenging work, by contrast, is engaging, intriguing, curiosity-provoking, enlightening, and purposeful.

Develop procedures for "buying time." Struggling students will sometimes need to continue working with current tasks after other students have completed their work. You may also need to guide these students to develop essential knowledge, understanding, and skills from previous years. You must first identify the knowledge, understanding, and skills that are truly *essential* to the student's continued growth and that the student has not yet developed. By focusing on genuinely nonnegotiable knowledge that the student must master and eliminating what would be nice to know if there were time, it is usually possible to identify a substantial amount of time for "working backward" on gaps in knowledge from previous years while still helping the student progress with current goals. Figure 6.6 suggests some mechanisms for focusing students' attention on nonnegotiable knowledge, understanding, and skills, both past and current.

Whichever strategies you use for this purpose, students must still be asked to do essential, proactively planned, sequentially offered, and consistently monitored work. These principles are imperative at all grade levels and in all content areas. Sometimes, coplanning or coteaching with a learning specialist can yield considerable benefits for both you and your students. Always remember, though, that "remediation" should not dominate a student's life in the classroom. All students need to work with powerful and engaging ideas and use essential skills to explore those ideas. All students need to apply essential skills to meaningful and relevant work and transfer powerful new ideas beyond the classroom. A primary focus on remediation rarely, if ever, lifts students up. It's much more likely to confine them to tedium in school and limit their horizons beyond the classroom (Bland, 2022).

Figure 6.6
Methods to "Buy Time" for Struggling Students to Build Foundational Learning

Strategy	Explanation
Learning Contracts, Menus, Centers, and Computer Programs	Instructional strategies such as these are designed to help teachers provide varied work for students around common topics, skills, or concepts. A student who needs additional practice with academic vocabulary in science, for example, may have a contract or learning menu focused on science vocabulary, whereas other students will focus on different content. These approaches also allow teachers to incorporate both current and past content into student assignments.
Regular Individual and Small-Group Instruction	It's important to plan consistent time to work with individuals or small groups who have learning gaps or who learn content with difficulty. This is a particularly efficient means of understanding students' needs, providing targeted instruction, and assessing student progress.
Alternative Homework Assignments	Continually attempting homework that is beyond a student's reach leads to frustration and confusion. If a particular homework assignment is inappropriate for a student, it is much wiser to give that student an assignment that helps them make progress with past learning gaps.
Scaffolded Assignments	It is often possible to create a scaffolded version of an assignment that other students can complete with little or no support. Scaffolding can include step-by-step directions, examples, "watch out for" warnings where students might get confused, hints written in the columns, content that is rewritten in more straightforward language, recorded directions or resource materials, and text in both English and a student's first language.
Double-Dipping	It is sometimes helpful for elementary students to work with a content area more than once a day. For example, a student might meet with two reading groups to practice decoding or comprehension skills. Some secondary school students can be placed in two periods of the same subject—in one, the teacher differentiates the content for students, and in the other, the teacher reinforces the goals of the first class by teaching the ideas in a different way, probing student thinking for understanding and misunderstanding and focusing on particularly complex skills. In the latter instance, the two class periods must be very tightly coordinated and aligned.

Routines for Keeping Track of Progress

Teachers in all classrooms have the responsibility to monitor student proficiency in relation to designated learning goals. A differentiated classroom varies only in that the teacher assumes students may sometimes work with different goals at different times or for varied lengths of time. It's not difficult to know who has mastered what in a differentiated classroom as long as the teacher is clear about the essential learning goals and has a system for monitoring student growth toward those goals. With a clear scope and sequence or delineation of what students should learn, a teacher can monitor a particular student's progress toward established goals, even if the student is working with different materials, on a different timetable, or with tasks at different levels of difficulty.

Figure 6.7 provides an example of a record-keeping system used in an elementary classroom to monitor student growth in the key elements of reading. Pages are alphabetized by student name, and each form is accompanied by several blank sheets of paper on which the teacher attaches or writes observations obtained in a variety of contexts. Even when students work with varied assignments, the teacher is able to readily monitor their progress toward common goals. Figure 6.8 (see p. 162) presents a similar example at a secondary level. There are also numerous online tools that can help teachers monitor and digitally keep track of student growth in essential knowledge, understanding, and skills.

An Important Reminder

School is a place of learning for students and teachers alike. Even though every procedure and routine in this book is valuable in providing structures that allow flexible teaching and learning, it makes no sense to teach students of any age to understand and implement all of them at once. Your goal should be to begin with the routines that seem the most fundamental to student success and introduce new ones as they are needed and as students are ready for them—polishing and revising as you go.

Similarly, teachers who are new to leading and managing a differentiated classroom need to see themselves as learners, too. For most teachers, it's overwhelming to think about planning, implementing, and supervising all of these routines at once. Teachers should accord themselves the privilege of learning over time, just as they do their students. Choose one or two routines you feel would be helpful to move your teaching forward. Plan for them carefully. Implement them when you feel ready. Study the results as you go. Take time to polish

Figure 6.7
Record of Reading Progress

Student: _____

1st Assessment Date: _____

2nd Assessment Date: _____

3rd Assessment Date: _____

4th Assessment Date: _____

Elements of Reading	#1	#2	#3	#4
Reading Strategies				
✓ skips unknown words and reads on				
✓ guesses what the word might be				
✓ starts over and reads the whole sentence				
✓ derives meaning from the pictures (or words)				
✓ uses beginning letter as a clue				
✓ asks for help				
Phonemic Awareness				
Concepts of Print				
Phonics				
Word Recognition				
Fluency				
Comprehension				

Teacher Comments:

#1	#2	#3	#4

Figure 6.8

Checklist of Writing Skills and Competencies

Student: _____ Date: _____ Evaluation: _____

Content and Expression
- ❏ Main idea is evident and appropriate.
- ❏ Details support key idea/argument.
- ❏ Descriptive details engage reader and extend ideas.
- ❏ Shows understanding of topic.
- ❏ Shows insight about topic.

Organization
- ❏ Effective title.
- ❏ Introduction establishes purpose.
- ❏ Logical flow of paragraphs.
- ❏ Logical flow of ideas within paragraphs.
- ❏ Effective transitions to guide reader.
- ❏ Conclusion summarizes/emphasizes key idea(s).

Style
- ❏ Word choice is appropriate for audience/topic.
- ❏ Word choice is precise for purpose.
- ❏ Vocabulary is varied and engaging.
- ❏ Sentences are complete.
- ❏ Sentences are clear.
- ❏ Sentence length varies.
- ❏ Sentence structure is varied.

Mechanics
- ❏ Subjects & verbs agree.
- ❏ Verb tenses are consistent.
- ❏ Subjects & objects agree.
- ❏ Plurals are used correctly.
- ❏ Capitalization is used correctly.
- ❏ End punctuation is correct.
- ❏ Commas are used correctly.
- ❏ Apostrophes are used correctly.
- ❏ Spelling is correct.

Teacher Comments:

and become comfortable with one routine or set of routines before you take on others.

If you pace yourself in a persistent pattern of growth, eventually you will not be able to recall what it was like to teach any other way. Not surprisingly, your students will learn the routines more rapidly at that point. In the meantime, however, be patient with yourself. Be a learner. Take one step, then another. Figure things out along with your students. Don't be afraid to stumble along the way. Most important, enjoy the journey.

7

Yes, But...
Common Sticking Points About Differentiation

In a real sense all life is interrelated. All men are caught in an inescapable network of mutuality, tied in a single garment of destiny. Whatever affects one directly affects all indirectly. I can never be what I ought to be until you are what you ought to be, and you can never be what you ought to be until I am what I ought to be. This is the interrelated structure of reality.

—Dr. Martin Luther King Jr.

Human beings seldom get excited about the need to make big changes in their lives—and teachers are human beings. In the face of evidence that we would fare better if we exercised more, we often assert that we simply don't have the time. Faced with the need to save for a rainy day, many of us declare that there simply is no margin in our budgets. Presented with evidence that student-focused teaching has multiple benefits for students and teachers, many teachers have a ready and substantial list of "yes, but..." statements at hand.

Reservations and Responses

Here are some common "yes, buts..." that we've heard... and that you may be holding in your own mind:

- I can't differentiate instruction because I have to cover the standards with everyone, and differentiation requires too much class time away from that.
- I can't differentiate instruction because the standardized test is not differentiated.
- I can't differentiate instruction because I'm already too busy and have absolutely no extra time in my life for planning differentiation.
- I can't differentiate instruction because I teach too many students.
- I can't differentiate instruction because I have only one textbook.
- I can't differentiate instruction because my classroom is too small.
- I can't differentiate instruction because it won't prepare students for college.
- I can't differentiate instruction because parents won't accept it.

The reality is, of course, that most of these "yes, buts..." are easily addressed.

I can't differentiate instruction because I have to cover the standards with everyone, and differentiation takes too much class time away from that. There are at least three issues with this argument that are important, if difficult, to consider. First, a curriculum should be much more than a list of standards. Second, a race to cover curriculum is highly unlikely to produce durable and transferable outcomes for students. Third, it does not, or need not, take more class time to differentiate instruction than it would take to teach a nondifferentiated lesson in which there is time for students to process what they are learning.

Envisioning curriculum as a list or set of standards is much like feeding young people vitamin tablets three times a day and believing that to be as nutritious or satisfying as eating meals that are appealing, varied, and healthy. It's like making the case that since people can now see images of most places on the planet via the internet, they have no need to travel beyond their own backyard. All three omit the human need for meaning, experience, and fulfillment.

Equating "coverage" of curriculum with either real teaching or actual learning overlooks two important and interconnected realities. First, learning doesn't happen *to* students; it happens *in* them. Passive learning is an oxymoron. The brain is not well suited to remembering large amounts of information for even a short time span, and certainly not for extended periods. When coverage is the goal of teaching, it is likely that the teacher is the only one who is truly learning—and even that is doubtful.

Second, learning requires sense making, or processing of information, ideas, and skills in order to integrate them into memory and to enable transfer of learning. For that reason, virtually every class period or lesson needs to include time for students to make sense of or come to "own" what the teacher is asking them to learn. Learning happens in those times when students are "on center stage" rather than when the teacher is "on stage." When we allow coverage to deplete time for student processing, we have lost touch with the meaning and mechanics of both teaching and learning.

Finally, if there is time during a class (as there should be) for students to process learning, then there is time to differentiate instruction. If students will have 15 minutes in today's class to work in small groups to solve a problem, try out a newly introduced form of self-expression, explain in a diagram why a science demonstration produced the results it produced, and so on, the work students do during that 15 minutes can be differentiated. In other words, it doesn't have to take more time for students to complete a differentiated assignment than the nondifferentiated version would require—and student outcomes should be more promising.

At the core of all three reasons why coverage is a highly questionable approach to teaching and learning is this: learning happens when an individual is *engaged* with what they are learning—that is, when the content seems interesting, relevant, worthwhile to the learner—and when the learner comes to *understand* the purpose and mechanics of content—its whys, whats, and hows. The terms *engagement* and *understanding* have, for many years, been used in the field of psychology to describe underpinnings of successful learning. Educational neuroscience uses the terms *meaning* and *sense* to note the brain's requirements for learning (Sousa & Tomlinson, 2018). The meaning of the two pairs of terms is the same. The two domains of research have drawn the same conclusion: to learn in ways that make us stronger, more productive, and better able to grapple with problems and issues, both known and unknown, requires student engagement (or meaning) as well as understanding (or sense) (Sousa & Tomlinson, 2018; Tomlinson, 2021). A "curriculum of coverage" rarely results in a learning environment that provides those critical conditions for durable and significant learning (Wiggins & McTighe, 2005).

I can't differentiate instruction because the standardized test is not differentiated. Differentiating curriculum and instruction makes it *more* likely, not *less*, that students will learn what we ask them to learn. The rare IEP aside, differentiation doesn't steer a classroom of students with varied learning needs toward a varied range of learning outcomes depending on individual students' perceived ability or current achievement level. What differentiation does is provide varied conditions conducive to helping students with a range of learning needs master the *same* set of learning outcomes. As one educator explained, differentiation provides different pathways through the same woods. Students who progressively succeed with learning throughout the months before a standardized test are more likely to perform well on the test than students who struggle within one-size-fits-all curriculum and instruction. In addition, these students are more likely to be able to approach the test with confidence and to work with it more seriously and hopefully. When standardized test prep either *becomes* the curriculum or dictates instruction, we have made a decision that is dangerously limiting for both teachers and learners.

I can't differentiate instruction because I'm already too busy and have absolutely no extra time in my life for planning differentiation. The idea is not to plan everything the way you always have and *then* plan differentiation on top of that. Rather, it is to plan instruction in a differentiated fashion from the outset. In addition, it's essential for teachers to pace themselves and move into new ways of thinking about teaching and learning at a rate that produces growth and change without being overwhelming.

Begin by using some strategies that take less time to plan: standing at the classroom door as students enter and leave so you can exchange brief comments with them, providing peer mentors to support newcomers to the class and English learners, giving students a choice of ways to work on an assignment or to express what they have learned, or meeting with small groups of students as other students complete assignments. Begin differentiating in just one subject, if you are an elementary teacher, or in just one class, if you are a secondary teacher. (It makes sense to begin with the subject or class in which students have the greatest need, but it makes sense in a different way to begin with the subject or class that is most comfortable for you.)

In differentiated classes, teachers ask students to take their own next steps every day. So ask that of yourself too. Go at a pace that challenges you but doesn't frustrate you. Just don't stand still. The good news is that, like any worthy skill set, the skills of differentiation become easier and more natural as you continue to develop them. In time, they become just how you do things in your role as a teacher.

I can't differentiate instruction because I teach too many students. We have heard this comment from teachers who have 5 or 6 students in their classroom as well as from those whose classrooms accommodate 50 students or more. It's hard not to advocate for smaller class sizes, but at the same time, we regularly see teachers with reduced class sizes who continue to teach just as they did when their classrooms were packed, as well as teachers with very large classes who work persistently and effectively to know their students and respond to their key needs.

Research on the impact of reducing class size is a mixed bag. There is little, if any, agreement on the number of students that is most beneficial in a class or the percentage of reduction necessary to make a difference in student learning. Some studies point to (generally small) achievement benefits for very young students in classes with greatly reduced class sizes, and other studies suggest reducing class size has a positive impact on achievement when the class is composed of vulnerable students (Bowe et al., 2017; Chen, 2022).

John Hattie (2017), whose meta-analysis of 1,000 education-focused meta-analyses considered 50,000 studies including 250 million students, ranked class size as 190th out of 256 possible positive influences on student achievement—not impressive!

Some policy analysts find that while decreasing class size is popular among parents and teachers, funding class size reduction eliminates expenditures on other initiatives that would likely have a greater impact on student achievement—for example, higher salaries for teachers, developing teacher expertise, and other conditions that would enable hiring larger numbers of highly prepared candidates (Chen, 2022; Hattie, 2009, 2012, 2017; Jepsen, 2015). Hattie (in Chen, 2022) reports that the key reason class size reduction does not have the impact we would imagine is that teachers generally do not change the way they teach when class sizes are reduced.

In the end, a decision about whether differentiation is possible given the number of students in your class should also factor in that this is the only 4th grade year (or kindergarten year, Algebra 1 year, and so on) your students will ever have. Waiting until we all have smaller class sizes to begin considering differentiation could be a long and costly wait. When we believe we cannot do something, we prove ourselves right, and when we believe we *can* do that same thing, we again prove ourselves right. Start with small steps. Build as you go. Like parenting or mastering a musical instrument or becoming an impressive basketball player, learning to differentiate instruction is a journey, not a moment. Our students need us to commit to the journey.

I can't differentiate instruction because I have only one textbook. There are countless materials available to teachers and students now other than the textbook. Many texts provide supplementary materials to support differentiation as well as varied modes of taking in knowledge and expressing learning. School media specialists are also valuable resources for matching materials to student needs. The internet is full of resources that support learning of particular content in a great variety of ways.

I can't differentiate instruction because my classroom is too small. It would be great to teach in a spatially generous setting, but many of us don't have that luxury. Again, a small room size doesn't seem to discourage teachers who mean to differentiate instruction—although those teachers would doubtless love to have a larger room—and a larger room does not seem to be an automatic catalyst for student-focused instruction. Ask your students to help you figure out ways to maximize the space you have. Be resourceful together!

I can't differentiate instruction because it won't prepare students for college. This "yes, but..." often reflects two different concerns. One is that if high school and even middle school students are not learning to listen to lectures, take notes, and figure out how to study for the kind of exams we presume they will experience in college, they will not be prepared for the way college classes are taught. The other concern is that differentiation mollycoddles students instead of preparing them for the hardships ahead.

There are at least two reasons to rethink those two assertions. First, schools should engage in developmentally appropriate instruction. Clearly, middle school students are not at the same developmental level as college students, and high school students aren't either. Effective differentiation absolutely prepares students for higher education by working to ensure that they learn the content, habits of mind, academic skills, and self-awareness necessary for continuing learning following whatever path they take beyond high school. There is little reason to assume that "academic boot camp" is the wisest route for preparing students for life after K–12.

Second, the image of the college professor who stands behind a podium and lectures for an hour or two or three at a time does not reflect reality in many post–high school institutions. Many colleges and universities offer extensive support services for students who have learning disorders, problems with attending or remaining still for extended periods, executive function challenges, and a wide range of physical challenges. Even colleges with large first-year classes offer lab sections or tutorials to support student success. More to the point, many colleges and universities provide ongoing (and often very high quality) support for faculty members in teaching practices that support the success of the full range of learners they instruct. A worthwhile book called *What the Best College Teachers Do* (Bain, 2004) finds that the best college teachers are not, in fact, lecturers who assume their job is to cover content and the job of their students is to figure it out from there. They recognize that teaching isn't just delivering lectures; it's doing anything they can to help and encourage students to learn—"creating conditions in which most, if not all, of our students will realize their potential to learn" (p. 173).

That sounds a great deal like differentiation, which seeks always to support students at their current points of development and to prepare them for the next chapter of their lives by helping them develop as whole human beings, not restrict learning in ways that do little to commend its appeal and value.

I can't differentiate instruction because parents won't accept it. Few parents recoil at the idea of a teacher who genuinely cares about the growth of their child and who is willing to invest in making sure each student has the most productive year possible. This is what differentiation aims to do. If you begin a conversation with a parent who questions differentiated instruction by explaining that your goal is to help their child learn as much and as efficiently as possible and that you are hoping they will be your partner in making that happen, you're not likely to meet resistance. In effectively differentiated classes, students feel more seen, accepted, and appropriately challenged. Those students generally go home in a positive state of mind. Seeing their children feel happy and productive is likely to make parents happy as well.

If you teach in a context where parents (and therefore, probably students) feel highly competitive, be ready to listen to their concerns and to answer in ways that respond to those concerns reasonably. When parents tell you their child is finding the work too easy, listen. Watch that student carefully. Parents know students in ways we cannot—especially early in a school year. Maybe the parents are correct. On the other hand, if more complex work results in anxiety or work of poor quality, be ready to talk with the parent about the stepwise process of learning. Skipping steps can result in long-term struggles. Help the parent understand that your goal is to help the student move forward smoothly and successfully, not to hold the student back. If parents of an advanced learner feel their child is being "punished" with work that is "harder" than what you assign to other students in the class, help the parents understand that your role is to ensure their child has the opportunity to grow, not march in place. Parents of a talented pianist would not accept a piano teacher who only asked the young person to play "age appropriate" pieces. Parents of a talented athlete would not accept a coach who refused to challenge their child in a way that would build athletic skills. In fact, parents should be distressed by situations in which teachers fail to recognize and develop a learner's strengths. In terms of challenge, the goal in a differentiated classroom is to have students work regularly at a level of challenge that pushes them a little too hard for comfort and to provide a support system that enables them to succeed with work that, at first, seems out of reach.

These "yes, buts..." are common, predictable, and understandable. They provide a safety net, a shield, in the face of a call to disrupt the generally comfortable routines we've established. To the degree that we can cling to them, we feel justified in our sense that this "differentiation thing" is impractical—at least in our own classrooms. Nevertheless, many teachers who initially have a "yes, but..." response grow increasingly uncomfortable in the face of student frustration and stagnation. Those teachers finally take the risk and implement student-focused approaches in their classroom, and they often have three realizations. First, their students are the beneficiaries of their efforts. Second, addressing their students' needs wasn't nearly as forbidding as they had assumed it would be. Third, they feel better about teaching and about themselves as teachers.

Incrementally (but steadily), these teachers learn to be responsive to the students they teach, and positive student outcomes encourage continued teacher development. Somewhere in this process, the "yes, buts..." cease to serve a purpose and become an artifact of the past. In other words, propelled by a sense of necessity and nurtured by a sense of accomplishment, many teachers answer their own concerns through increasingly effective practices.

Not all "yes, but..." statements are knee-jerk excuses that typify an early response to change. Some are more complex and confounding. They persist even as teachers make changes toward effective differentiation in their classrooms. Two of the more challenging concerns involve students who bring complex challenges of their own into the classroom and grading in a differentiated classroom. The remainder of this chapter provides some thoughts and guidance on these two areas, both of which have implications for leading and managing a differentiated classroom.

"But My Students Are Different"

A number of teachers who genuinely desire to provide all of their students with the opportunity to access excellence and maximize their capacities are held back by worries that some, many, or all of them can't handle the sort of flexible and collaborative classroom that differentiation advocates. In essence, their response is something like, "Differentiation would be wonderful, but I don't think you know the students *I* teach." The comment is not so much a dismissive "yes, but…" as it is a real sense that at least some of their students are not now capable of making decisions in their own self-interest, collaborating, or even following general guidelines for classroom civility.

It is important to note that virtually all teachers, at any given time, teach some students whose deprivation, anger, discouragement, disillusionment, alienation, frustration, or trauma is so great that it is difficult, if not impossible, for them to exhibit sustained contributions to a classroom community. Working with only a few of these students can be both challenging and gut-wrenching. When a school or class is heavily populated with students whose lives are markedly off-course in one or more ways, the challenge feels massive. There is no formula for teachers to follow in such settings. These classrooms demand from the teacher the highest levels of empathy, persistence, thought, and creativity.

Still, there are principles that derive from both research and effective classroom practice to guide teachers who work with deeply disaffected or emotionally challenged students. We'll share a few of these principles in the following sections, including some general ideas about leading and guiding students whose lives are more difficult than a young person's should have to be, and we'll share some guidelines for working with particular groups of students who may experience and create difficulties in the classroom.

In most classes, a majority of students are ready, willing, and able to be part of a learning community that is safe, welcoming, challenging, supportive, and responsive to their needs. There will likely be a few students who sometimes need additional support and reminders about procedures and guidelines. In such classes, the major challenge of leading and managing a classroom comes from one or a very few students who consistently push against the norms. In other classrooms, a majority of students do not affiliate with school, and the climb for teacher and students to achieve an orderly, flexible classroom is much steeper. The guidelines below are relevant to both contexts, but they will likely need to be implemented differently in the two contexts.

Invest heavily in establishing strong teacher–student connections and building trust. Make sure the classroom feels safe, welcoming, and supportive to each learner. Examine your own mindset, biases, and determination to provide dynamic learning opportunities for each of your students. Whenever possible, learn each student's name and its correct pronunciation before the first day the student comes to your class. Meet and observe each student with unconditional positive regard—your belief that a student doesn't have to be something or do something to earn your approval (Gobir, 2021). Let your students know you want to get to know them so that you can teach them more effectively—and simply because you think a bonus of your role as a teacher is learning about the people you'll spend time with during the year. Help them get to know you.

Have interesting things for your students to do from the first moments of class, and work to be sure students see themselves in what they are learning. Plan for student engagement. Study your students consistently to begin to understand what seems to work for them as individuals and as a group and plan accordingly. Ask them to tell you what they think makes a great class and what they wish teachers wouldn't do. Ask for student input whenever that is feasible—and honor what you hear. Let students know that you want to earn their trust, and make doing that a priority from the outset of the year.

Chad Prather, a colleague of ours, has taught almost solely in urban settings where many students have learned to distrust adults in school. He is white; most of his high school history students are Brown or Black. His thinking and planning for the early days of a school year is evident in the passage below.

> Trust is cultivated over time; it does not just happen. The start matters, though. Week 1 is a big deal. I go into it every year wanting to lay the groundwork for some serious trust-building, and I tend to feel really good about it... right up to the moment when we get to the "Rules and Management" slide. I struggle every year with this slide. There's something fundamentally awkward about saying, "I am trying to build trust, but I am going to manage you, and here are rules for you to follow." I recover quickly, though, because I'm confident that what has happened in the past will probably happen again: Somewhere along the line, something in most of my students will click toward me, and I will click toward them, and eventually most of us will be clicking together.
>
> But I want more. I want my students, all of them, to start our time together feeling that they're on the cusp of something different. That in this classroom, they do not need to feel policed or compelled into compliance with more rules. I want them to get that this classroom will be a place of co-ownership and mutual accountability—a place of agreements, not rules, and a place where the

norms won't only be normative to me. I want them to see that I'm not asking for obedience but partnership. (This may feel awkward, too, because how often have they felt like partners with their teachers? But this will be a different kind of awkward, more hopeful and inviting.)

How do I invite students into partnership with me? They hardly know me. And let's be honest: I look like lots of the people who haven't had their backs in the past. Despite 16 years as a teacher, I am still struggling to know how to do this—how to shift from rule-giving to agreement-making. Fortunately, I have a colleague who does this work beautifully, and I have learned over time that asking for help is liberating. (in Tomlinson, 2021, p. 250)

Chad invites his associate, who is known to and respected by his students, to lead a discussion of what agreements they feel would benefit the members of this class. She asks the students and Chad to sit with her in a circle. She begins a discussion based on their experiences and shares some that were positive in her development. She provides time for thinking. She points to the different perspectives she's hearing from the students. She affirms the values they express and moves slowly from those values to agreements by posing four questions: How should teachers treat students? How should students treat teachers? How should students treat one another? How should everyone treat the space they will share?

The pace is slow—the process takes multiple class periods. In time, the group has constructed its first agreement. "Teachers will not judge students for their emotions. They will try to understand what is going on and create opportunities for upset students to re-engage. If the students can't or choose not to, then they will be respectfully dismissed" (Tomlinson, 2021, p. 252). Chad reflects that by the time students had considered all four questions and the process ended, he and his students felt like partners in the work they had completed, and he felt ready to roll out the process in his other classes.

Don't lower your expectations for students. This is just as true when the focus is behavior, classroom participation, and self-awareness as a learner as it is when the focus is cognitive outcomes.

In regard to cognitive development, there is more than ample evidence that "remediating" students often further hobbles them (e.g., Berger et al., 2014; Hopfenberg & Levin, 2008). What they need to succeed are high expectations, acceleration that focuses on essential content to propel them forward, and support for the journey (Hopfenberg & Levin, 2008).

In regard to meaningful participation in a classroom community, the same principle holds. Of all students in a school who need to learn the skills of academic self-awareness, peer collaboration, and community membership, those who need them most are those who are most alienated from the skills and the promise they represent. The path to achieving these skills with disaffected students is not easy, linear, straightforward, or quick. Nonetheless, you cannot serve disenfranchised students well unless you keep your eyes on the destination they need to reach and guide them steadily in that direction. In other words, we fail students when we look at what we believe they cannot do and lower our sights accordingly rather than look at what they need to do and continually try to lift them to that level.

Marva Collins (1992), an African American educator known as a champion of equity and excellence for students of color and students living in poverty, says she discouraged her students from being average, adding that she believed each of her students could learn significantly so long as she did not teach them that they could not. She summarizes that philosophy:

> When our children walk in the door, I say, "Welcome to success. Say goodbye to failure, because you are not going to fail. You are here to win, and if I have to care more about you than you care about you, that's the way it will be." It doesn't matter what kind of disciplinary problems they had in previous schools, there are with us to succeed. We will not let them fail. (p. 16)

Move slowly but persistently toward helping all students work productively and create quality work. You may (or may not) introduce ideas and routines more slowly in settings where many students exhibit challenging behavior. You may (or may not) use the routines for briefer periods in a class or day. You may need to practice and model routines more frequently. You may have more false starts and disappointments along the way. What you should *not* do is accept the inevitability of a "tight-ship classroom," which, by its nature, communicates to students a lack of trust, eliminates the opportunity for students to engage with meaningful content and with one another, and deprives students of the chance to take control of their lives as learners.

Learn from the "warm demanders." It's often the case that students who are perennially disruptive in one class work quite well in another. The difference—particularly for students from low-income or African American backgrounds—is often that teachers in the classes where students are successful are "warm demanders" (Alexander, 2016; Berry, 2021; Bondy & Ross, 2008; Ware, 2006). These teachers have two critical traits that may seem paradoxical but actually send important signals to students—especially those whose feelings about school are ambivalent or negative. First, the teachers are clear and unequivocal about expectations for behavior and work. Said otherwise, they don't put up with nonsense in the classroom. At the same time, however, they communicate to students their unconditional acceptance, unwavering belief in each student's capacity to succeed, and full partnership in the goal of achieving success. In some cultures, parents are direct or even blunt in stating expectations and correcting misbehavior. For students from these backgrounds, such directness signals adult caring, and the "warm demander" fits that profile. Even students whose cultural expectations are for a more subdued form of communication may benefit from this clarity if they lack the internal structures necessary to make good judgments on their own behalf and if the demands are enveloped in the warmth of understanding and acceptance. Corita Kent, a graphic artist and author, once noted that a friend is someone who loves you just as you are and pays you the compliment of expecting you to become something better. Warm demanders do just that. In the process, they provide the external structures necessary to survive the moment and the guidance necessary to ultimately create internal structures that lead to self-direction.

Remember that young people will generally succeed if they can. Susan Craig (2008, 2017) and Ross Greene (2014, 2021a, 2021b) are two of many experts working with disaffected learners who remind us that young people find it more satisfying to succeed than to fail. For this reason, most students will almost always do what is in their best interest if they have the skills to do so. Understanding this will help you think about an event or about the classroom in general from the student's perspective (and will help you avoid the trap of blaming the student). The two pertinent questions become "What academic and personal skills does this student need to develop to handle situations like this?" and "What can I do to help this student develop those skills and regain agency in their life?"

Trauma involves experiences that exceed one's capacity to cope. Such experiences include but are not limited to impacts of race, sexual orientation, disability, poverty, physical abuse, and immigration status. As a result of trauma, students are unable to access the brain cortex—the area of the brain in which higher-order thinking takes place. Essentially, their learning is held hostage by relentless fear and hyperarousal that derail the focus needed to achieve academically. The tension and anxiety are magnified as teachers and peers look at them as problems to be dealt with—as if they were willfully creating classroom disruptions—rather than understanding that they are young people in acute need of safety and support (Craig, 2017).

Aim to look at each of your students with empathy—to try to see the world through their eyes. Try to understand the circumstances in their lives that make growing up more challenging than it ought to be and to offer each student trustworthy support, including the skills and habits of mind they will need for the journey they're taking. When things go off course, remember that the road to success is never without pitfalls and perils. Be there to help the student think about "the derailing," to understand what went wrong, and to craft a plan for resuming the journey with surer footing.

Invest heavily in trying to understand the cause of a student's misbehavior. Begin with the understanding that behavior is communication and protest. Young people, especially, often don't have the words to explain negative experiences they have suffered, and so they "speak" in the only way they can express the hurt—through behavior. A student may experience racial animosity on a daily basis, live with the deprivation that accompanies poverty, feel rejected or be bullied by peers, be frustrated by work that is out of reach, be underchallenged and bored on a daily basis, be hungry, see school as irrelevant, find it impossible to sit and listen as much as is required, have a chronically ill family member, or be a victim of abuse or neglect. The gamut of possibilities is long and wide. It can be very helpful to understand the origin of counterproductive behavior in order to address it in a way that helps the student make sense of life rather than in a way that further complicates life for the student. Greene (2014, 2021a) reminds us that we don't need a diagnosis to address maladaptive behavior, because a diagnosis doesn't yield any strategies for moving ahead. Understanding the world from the student's point of view, however, can be immensely useful in helping you determine potentially beneficial next steps away from the problem and toward working with the student for a constructive and long-lasting solution. From that point, you will be better positioned to help the student understand their behavior and to develop responses that are increasingly positive and productive.

Be proactive. Craig (2008) recalls being a young teacher who was focused on student accountability for behavior. One day, she complained about a student who was regularly disruptive, and a colleague turned the tables and asked, "What can you change about your teaching practice to help this child be more successful?" (p. 13). Recall some key tenets of this book and of differentiation. Students work more productively and successfully when the classroom feels safe, when they feel valued and supported, when the work teachers ask them to do is at an appropriate challenge level, when the work is personally and/or culturally relevant (and therefore interesting), and when there are opportunities to learn and express learning in ways that are efficient for them. Working diligently to ensure that these conditions prevail in the classroom eliminates many problems. A veteran teacher once noted, "If the classroom system works for the kid, the kid generally quits working the system." However, be cognizant of patterns associated with a student's problematic behavior. You might increase the likelihood of a good outcome by seating the student in a particular place, providing step-by-step directions rather than a long paragraph, reminding the student of a goal they set, assigning students to groups rather than risking the high likelihood that a particular student will be the last one chosen by a group, allowing a student extra time to get organized before beginning a task, ensuring opportunities for students to move around as they learn, or having a "Quiet Zone" in the classroom where a student can go to regain calm when tensions are mounting. As in all aspects of teaching, planning for success and planning to avoid failure are powerful tools. It's important to recall that the foundation of student success is nearly always a strong teacher–student connection built on mutual respect, empathy, and trust.

Pick your battles. Don't let smaller issues become flash points. When a student exhibits a negative behavior, try some small, gentle moves like these:

- Look at the student with bewilderment. The message you want to send is that the student is wonderful but what the student is doing is *not* wonderful, so you're confused.
- Tap on an item that shouldn't be on a table or desk as you continue to pass by. This gives the student an opportunity to save face and get it right.
- Assume intelligence by simply saying, "You know what to do." This tells the student you know they are smart and you don't need to tell them what to do next.
- State a fact like, "Your desk has stuff under it" or "There are things you need to do before we begin our next activity." This allows you to avoid nagging or embarrassing a student.
- Ask a quick question like, "What should you be doing now?" When a student knows what to do, this allows them to take positive action without your telling the student what to do (Ervin, 2022).

Don't take negative behavior personally. There's a powerful moment in the movie *Stand and Deliver* when the teacher hands a book to a student only to have the student intentionally let the book fall to the floor. In a single gesture, the teacher picks the book up, opens it to the correct place, and continues to explain what the student needs to do. By refusing to allow the student's challenge to escalate, the teacher kept the focus on learning and maintained a positive interaction with the student. Keep the focus on learning whenever possible. Don't become a co-combatant with the student. Someone has to be the adult, and that someone is you.

Don't be afraid to delay handling a tense situation. Of course, challenging behavior must be handled swiftly if student safety is an issue, but most of the time, it's both possible and wise to delay dealing with a behavior issue (Greene, 2014, 2021a, 2021b). You may simply say to a student (privately, if at all possible), "I see that you are angry right now and it's difficult for you to concentrate on your work. I want to talk with you in a little while about this, but for right now, please write about how you're feeling in your journal." The immediate prescription for the student's next step will vary, of course, depending on their specific needs. The intention is to allow some time to think before you address the issue. Eliminating "heat" from a tense situation allows "light" to enter the picture.

Demonstrate empathy and respect to identify solutions to a problem. When the time is right, talk with the student privately and with the goal of finding a reasonable and acceptable solution to the problem. Greene (2008) suggests beginning conversations with comments such as "I've noticed that you're not getting your homework done. Help me know what's up" and "Talk about what happened earlier today when you were so angry with Charles. I need to understand how you were feeling." As the conversation progresses, guide it toward a problem-solving mode. Say something like, "Let's figure out together how to address this. What do you think we can do to avoid this problem again?" Ultimately, the goal is to develop a series of steps that the student will take and you will support to eliminate, or at least minimize, the issue. Finally, you might end the conversation with a comment such as "Thank you for trusting me enough to tell me how you feel and for working with me to find a solution we can use." Along the way, it's important to be sure you both understand three things: the problem that evoked the negative behavior, that there has been an opportunity to explore that problem and a potential solution in some depth, and when a peer or other individual has been harmed or wronged by the student's behavior, how the student might go about righting the wrong.

It may appear to some that this approach to maladaptive behavior is "too easy" on the student or that it "lets the student off the hook." In truth, this approach involves two elements central to differentiation: teaching and leadership. It helps students understand themselves better, develop the insights and skills necessary for continued personal and academic growth, and establish the kind of trust that's required to follow a leader to a better place. Discipline implies teaching and learning; punishment does not, and empowering students to address and correct their own behavior is more effective than punishing negative behavior—in both the short and long term (Smith et al., 2015). When a student's behavior is significantly disruptive or dangerous and must be punished, it is still important to use interactions with the student as a teaching/learning opportunity.

"But Grading Requirements Don't Work with Differentiation"

A discussion about grading and report cards seems somehow unrelated to classroom management, yet the classroom is a system and all of its elements are interdependent.

Confusion about grading and differentiation is rarely an easily dismissed "yes, but…" excuse. Rather, it usually reflects genuine concern by teachers who work diligently to teach responsively to student strengths and needs but feel stymied by an apparent dissonance between the philosophy and goals of a differentiated classroom and those of grading. One teacher notes, "For nine weeks, I play the role of encourager, coach, and advocate. Then, on the last day of the nine weeks when grade reports go out, I become the judge. My students feel the change of roles as acutely as I do. It makes me feel like a fraud."

Those teachers worry that grading, as schools typically practice it, seems structured to be punitive to students who struggle, to reward students who are highly able and often coast to success (and damage those who are not), and to erode teacher–student trust. Alternatively, they worry that, somehow, differentiation requires a teacher to "jiggle" grades so that struggling students receive elevated grades for lesser goals. They are then concerned that those grades will be misinterpreted by parents, teachers, and counselors at the next level of schooling. A colleague of ours who is an expert in measurement and grading often remarks that there is no problem inherent to reconciling grading and differentiation. Rather, she says, our grading practices are such a mess that they make everything a problem. All indications are that she's correct.

There is no intrinsic conflict between sound grading practices and the philosophy of differentiation. What teachers perceive to be issues typically arise because grading practices are misaligned with best-practice grading, not because best-practice grading and differentiation are misaligned. The following principles and practices of grading are widely recommended by experts in the field of measurement and grading (e.g., Brookhart, 2017; Dimich et al., 2022; Earl, 2013; Guskey, 1994, 2020; Guskey & Brookhart, 2019; O'Connor, 2017, 2022; Tomlinson & Moon, 2013; Wiggins, 1993). As you read and think about them, consider the degree to which they support or undercut the goals of differentiation.

Grading is one moment in a long progression of assessment decisions. Perhaps the most common question about differentiation asked by teachers from all grade levels, subject areas, and countries is "Could you talk about assessment and differentiation?" We've learned to follow up with "Explain what you mean by assessment." Nearly always, the answer is "I mean grading. I don't know how to grade differentiation."

We point out that *grading* and *assessment* are not synonyms. Assessment is (or should be) a process of finding out where students are relative to key goals at a particular time and over time via formative assessment, with the goal of adapting instruction to support the student's efforts to learn more successfully. Grading is the periodic, somewhat public statement about a student's performance at designated intervals, and it will be more honest, useful, and accurate if it is an outgrowth of appropriate cycles of formative assessment and differentiated instruction.

The nature of a teacher's decisions about assessment will affect grading. For many teachers, assessment means giving enough tests and recording enough grades so they can defend a student's final grade at the end of a marking period. This conception of assessment invites "gotcha teaching." Differentiation advocates for a different perspective. Pre-assessment and ongoing formative assessment become mechanisms to inform teacher planning, create a match between student needs and classroom instruction, provide helpful feedback to students on their progress, and help students develop agency as learners. Pre-assessments should never be graded. Assignments that are used to generate formative data are rarely graded and then only with advance notice. The emphasis in formative assessment is providing feedback to students that acknowledges their progress and points to next steps in the learning process. In this way, ongoing assessment helps students understand learning goals, trace their progress toward those goals, and learn without the anxiety that often accompanies graded work so that when graded assessments *do* occur, students are more likely to be prepared or to know how to prepare. Very different classroom climates result when a teacher sees the need for students to practice before they are "measured" and envisions the assessment process as largely informative, as opposed to as a series of grading opportunities.

Instruction should be differentiated. The purpose of instruction is to do what's necessary to help each learner succeed. As teachers become more proficient with using what they learn about students through observation, conversation, and formative assessment to effectively address their readiness, interests, and learning preferences, an array of benefits occur. Students' achievement rises, and they begin to develop more of a growth mindset about themselves as learners—which contributes to their continuing investment in learning. Further, "grade trauma" diminishes not because a teacher awards extra points for "trying hard" (which should not occur), but because student achievement merits a higher grade.

Assessments can be differentiated. Effective assessments enhance the likelihood that students can truly demonstrate what they know, understand, and are able to do. The learning targets (also known as KUDs) that an assessment is designed to measure should *not* be differentiated except in the case of students with IEPs. However, it is allowable, for example, to provide some students more time to complete an assessment. Assessments that offer more than one way to demonstrate mastery are likely to enable more students to better show what they have learned. In addition, when teachers use more than one—or more than one form of—summative assessment (for example, right-answer assessments and performance assessments), more students are likely to have the opportunity to provide a more accurate accounting of what they have learned. Learning is multifaceted, and effective assessment plans take this reality into account.

Grading should stem from, not dictate, effective assessment practices. Too often in schools, the tail wags the dog in terms of grading. For example, we say, "I'm required to have at least 10 grades in my grade book each marking period, so I have to grade everything." We also say, "How can I document that I have provided specific feedback to students on their progress and guided them in setting personal goals for their work at least 10 times?" Finally, we might say, "I can't communicate anything but a single letter grade because the report card won't let me." In reality, we should ask, "What do we need to do in terms of reporting to benefit student achievement? What mechanisms, including but not limited to the report card, can support us in doing that?"

Grades should be based on clear and specific learning goals. When a teacher clearly articulates precisely what students must know, understand, and be able to do as a result of the unit and as a result of each segment of learning in the unit, there's a much better chance that goals, instruction, and assessments will all be aligned. Likewise, the likelihood of student success rises because expectations for students are clear, instruction is focused squarely on those expectations, and assessments are crafted to determine each student's proficiency with those expectations.

Simple as this sounds, such alignment is uncommon. Using a "backward design" process to ensure a curriculum/instruction/assessment match contributes directly to student achievement and makes "the moment of grading" more transparent—and more honest (Wiggins & McTighe, 2005).

Evidence that contributes to grading should be valid. A grade should communicate clearly and directly what a student knows, understands, and can do in comparison to stated goals at a particular time. No doubt a result of hand-me-down grading practices, teachers subtract points from tests because students forget to write their names on the paper, add points to grades because students complete extra credit projects that are only tangentially related to essential outcomes, tweak grades because students are nice or difficult, lower grades because students don't turn in homework (even though they might make a near-perfect grade on the final assessment), use zeros as a grade, and commonly assign a "mean" average as a final grade. All of these are forms of grade fog. That is, they obscure an accurate picture of the student's real achievement.

A nonnegotiable, meaningful grade is clear communication of student status relative to essential goals. Eliminating "fog-inducing" elements (such as the ones discussed earlier in this chapter) from grades also helps students chart a course to success and maintains student–teacher trust.

Students should be graded on clear criteria, not norms. When students compete against one another in a classroom, it very quickly becomes evident who the winners and losers will be. When they compete against clearly delineated criteria, however, every student has a chance for success. Thus, best-practice grading and differentiation support a "*J* curve," in which all students have the possibility of earning good grades. This is in opposition to a bell-shaped curve, in which only a few students can really succeed (Tomlinson & McTighe, 2006). Consider whether you would prefer a surgeon whose practice is based on a *J* curve or one who literally operates on a bell-shaped curve.

Grade later in a cycle rather than earlier. Schools generally allot a six- to nine-week period for students to develop proficiency with a given set of content goals. This decision suggests that it will take roughly that amount of time for students to achieve those goals, yet we typically begin to grade students on the content early in the marking period and average the early grades with summative grades to yield final report card grades. The result is that students hear from teachers, "I'm so sorry your grades were low early in the marking period. You made an *A* on your final, but your early grades pulled that down to a *B–*."

A summative assessment should be just that—summative. It's of little significance that it took a student the entire marking period to learn the essential knowledge; what should matter most is that the student is finally able to demonstrate proficiency. If we adhered to the practice of grading later in a cycle rather than earlier, we would encourage persistence (and a growth mindset) in struggling students who need additional time to learn and in advanced students who may fear tackling work that challenges them will result in lower status.

Report key elements of learner development, but report them separately. It's often difficult to know quite what a grade means. As teachers, we are inclined to report one grade that includes student achievement, a bit about compliance, and a bit about work habits. The result is that the grade is "mushy." It communicates poorly and does little to further student achievement.

There are three elements that teachers in a differentiated classroom need to keep in mind for students and their parents: achievement or performance, habits of mind or process, and growth or progress (Guskey, 1994, 2020). An achievement grade should reflect what a student knows, understands, and can do at a given time relative to stated goals. A grade for habits of mind should indicate the contribution a student makes to their own success. Does the student persist in the face of difficulty, ask for help when needed, revise work to improve its quality, set and pursue important academic goals, accept challenges, and look at issues from varied perspectives? A grade focused on student growth should stem from evidence that a student has or has not exhibited measurable progress toward established goals. These three elements should *not* be merged into a single grade. Rather, they should be distinct entities that work together to convey a critical message: people who work effectively will grow, and persistent growth is the key to achieving and exceeding academic goals. This is the core of a growth mindset. Sadly, it is seldom a vital part of teacher–student, teacher–parent, or parent–student conversations.

The ability to keep all three elements in the foreground of teacher, student, and parent thinking would do a great deal to propel student learning in a positive direction. It would also set the stage for continued success in life. Ideally, report cards would provide opportunities to describe these three key areas separately (achievement/performance, habits of mind/process, and growth/progress). Indeed, some report cards do this, but many do not. (If there is only space for one grade on a report card, it must be the student's achievement/performance grade.) The absence of boxes on a report card, however, should not eliminate the possibility of a teacher monitoring and reporting on all three elements. Teachers who understand the interconnectedness and importance of all three elements in student development can do the following:

- Talk with parents and students about all three aspects of student work at the beginning of the year, throughout the year, and at parent–teacher conferences.
- Have students keep ongoing records of all three aspects of their learning.
- Institute parent–student conferences to assess student development in all three areas.
- Add an addendum to a report card in the form of a prose statement or checklist.
- Email a three-part report to parents at the end of each marking period.

Teachers who lead for differentiation do many things to shape classroom culture on behalf of student achievement. Publicly valuing and ensuring that others understand the value of productive work habits and achievement is an extraordinarily important contribution teachers make to classrooms in which every student is expected to work hard, grow, and succeed.

In an effectively differentiated classroom, support for student achievement does *not* include modifying an achievement grade so it appears that a student has mastered content when they have not—and should not reward students for "excellence" in the absence of honest personal challenge and struggle. Support for student success stems from a growth mindset teacher; a classroom environment designed and nurtured to build a community in which all students support one another's achievement; a high-quality curriculum that engages students in the difficult work of learning; ongoing assessment that informs the next steps in the learning process (and that incorporates the best practices for assessment and grading noted earlier in this chapter); and instruction that is responsive to students' varied readiness levels, interests, and learning preferences. Under these conditions, grading flows appropriately and naturally.

Concluding Thoughts

We began this book by saying that what lay ahead was aspirational. We'd like to end the book with the same thoughts. Between the two of us, we have a combined teaching experience of more than 80 years and have taught preschool, elementary school, high school, undergraduate, master's, and doctoral students.

We understand that teaching is a devilishly difficult profession, made more so by external mandates to achieve the delusional—that is, to ensure that all students reach the same point of mastery of an unwieldy amount of content on the same day, and to demonstrate that mastery under the same conditions.

We know that students' lives have always been complex, and we are keenly aware that the complexity of students' lives is growing exponentially as a result of myriad confounding factors. We know that teachers are responsible for a greater variety of learners with a greater diversity of needs than ever before. We know there is not enough time in the day, not enough days in the week, and not enough weeks in the year to do what teachers need to do. We also know there would be a severe lack of energy to teach additional hours, days, or weeks if they *were* part of the school calendar.

Nevertheless, we also know that every student who enters every classroom will be enhanced or diminished by the collective attitudes, decisions, and practices of the teachers. We know that every young life that is redeemed by learning is an individual and a collective victory. Likewise, we know that every young life that is scarred by school is an individual and a collective tragedy. We know that contemporary schools and teachers need to develop beyond passive acceptance of what was "good enough" in the past. We know that this can only happen when teachers aspire to do their very best and, in the process, create better ways to ignite the spark of genius found in every human being with the flint of real learning.

It is not our expectation that teachers can read a book, flip a switch, and magically transform their teaching. Rather, we believe that there are teachers who aspire to understand the art and science of teaching a little better each day, who are willing to take the risk of confronting the effectiveness of the work they do in the lives of each student in their care, and who are courageous enough to make small and large decisions each day based on benefits to their students—individually and as a whole. It is to those teachers we offer the accumulated insights that make up this book.

We know teachers transform lives. We know because we have had the great fortune of being their students. We know because we continue to learn from aspirational teachers—one step at a time, day after year after decade—building careers and lives as they go. This breed of teacher is always more excited than daunted by what lies ahead. We hope you'll join up!

Yes, But...

I teach in a four-wall box of drab proportions,
But choose to make it a place that feels like home.
I see too many students to know them as they need to be known,
But refuse to let that render them faceless in my mind.
I am overcome with the transmission of a canon I can scarcely recall myself,
But will not represent learning as a burden to the young.
I suffer from a poverty of time,
And so will use what I have to best advantage those I teach.
I am an echo of the way school has been since forever,
But will not agree to perpetuate the echo another generation.
I am told I am as good a teacher as the test scores I generate,
But will not allow my students to see themselves as data.
I work in isolation,
And am all the more determined to connect my students with the world.
I am small in the chain of power,
But have the power to change young lives.
There are many reasons to succumb,
And thirty reasons five times a day to succeed.
Most decisions about my job are removed from me.
Except the ones that matter most.

References

Alexander, M. (2016, April 13). The warm demander: An equity approach. *Edutopia*. https://www.edutopia.org/blog/warm-demander-equity-approach-matt-alexander

Aronson, J., Fried, C., & Good, C. (2002). Reducing the effects of stereotype threat on African American college students by shaping theories of intelligence. *Journal of Experimental Social Psychology, 38*(2), 113–125.

Bain, K. (2004). *What the best college teachers do.* Harvard University Press.

Beane, J. (2005). *A reason to teach: Creating classrooms of dignity and hope.* Heinemann.

Berger, R. (2003). *An ethic of excellence: Building a culture of craftsmanship with students.* Heinemann.

Berger, R., Rugen, L., & Woodfin, L. (2014). *Leaders of their own learning: Transforming schools through student-engaged assessment.* Jossey-Bass.

Berry, R. (2021, March 21). Three ways being a "warm demander" is culturally responsive and supports students' mathematical identity and agency. *Corwin Connect.* https://corwin-connect.com/2021/03/three-ways-being-a-warm-demander-is-culturally-responsive-and-supports-students-mathematical-identity-and-agency/

Berwick, C. (2019, August 9). Is it time to detrack math? *Edutopia.* https://www.edutopia.org/article/it-time-detrack-math

Bishop, P., & Harrison, L. (2021). *The successful middle school: This we believe.* Association for Middle Level Education.

Bland, J. A. (2022, August 31). Back to school: 10 steps schools and districts can take to address new and ongoing COVID-19 challenges. Learning Policy Institute. https://learningpolicyinstitute.org/blog/covid-back-to-school-10-steps-address-covid-19-challenges

Bondy, E., & Ross, D. (2008, September). The teacher as warm demander. *Educational Leadership, 66*(1), 54–58.

Bowe, J., Magnuson, K., Schindler, H., Duncan, G., & Yoshikawa, H. (2017). A meta-analysis of class sizes and ratios in early childhood programs: Are thresholds of quality associated with greater impacts on cognitive, achievement, and socioemotional outcomes? *Educational Evaluation and Policy Analysis, 31*(3), 407–428.

Boykin, A., & Noguera, P. (2011). *Creating the opportunity to learn: Moving from research to practice to close the achievement gap.* ASCD.

Brighton, C. M., Hertberg, H. L., Moon, T. R., Tomlinson, C. A., & Callahan, C. M. (2005). *The feasibility of high-end learning in a diverse middle school.* National Research Center on the Gifted and Talented.

Brookhart, S. (2017). *How to use grading to improve learning.* ASCD.

Brookhart, S., & Rasooli, A. (2021, July). Planning for fair groupwork. *Educational Leadership, 78*(9). https://www.ascd.org/el/articles/planning-for-fair-group-work

Bruner, J. (1996). *The culture of education.* Harvard University Press.

Chen, G. (2022, May 20). Smaller class sizes: Pros and cons. *Public School Review.* https://www.publicschoolreview.com/blog/smaller-class-sizes-pros-and-cons

Cohen, E., & Lotan, R. (2014). *Designing group work: Strategies for the heterogeneous classroom* (3rd ed.). Teachers College Press.

Collins, M. (1992). *Ordinary children, extraordinary teachers.* Hampton Roads Publishing.

Collins, M., & Amabile, T. (1999). Motivation and creativity. In R. J. Sternberg (Ed.), *Handbook of creativity* (pp. 297–312). Cambridge University Press.

Council of Chief State School Officers. (2013, April). Interstate Teacher Assessment and Support Consortium InTASC Model Core Teaching Standards and Learning Progressions for Teachers 1.0: A resource for ongoing teacher development. https://ccsso.org/sites/default/files/2017-12/2013_INTASC_Learning_Progressions_for_Teachers.pdf

Craig, S. (2008). *Reaching and teaching children who hurt: Strategies for your classroom.* Paul H. Brookes.

Craig, S. (2017). *Trauma-sensitive schools: Promoting resiliency and healing, grades 6–12.* Teachers College Press.

Csikszentmihalyi, M. (1990). *Flow: The psychology of optimal experience.* HarperCollins.

Cummings, M. (2020, February 12). Study shows race, gender affect teachers' perceptions of students' ability. *Yale News.* https://news.yale.edu/2020/02/12/study-shows-race-gender-affect-teachers-perceptions-students-ability

Dack, H., & Tomlinson, C. (2015, March). Inviting all students to learn. *Educational Leadership, 72*(6), 10–15.

Darling-Hammond, L. (2001). Inequality in teaching and schooling: How opportunity is rationed to students of color in America. In B. D. Smedley, A. Y. Smith, L. Colburn, & C. H. Evans, *The right thing to do, the smart thing to do: Enhancing diversity in the health professions: Summary of the Symposium on Diversity in Health Professions in Honor of Herbert W. Nickens, MD.* National Institutes of Health. https://www.ncbi.nlm.nih.gov/books/NBK223640/

Darling-Hammond, L. (2009). *The flat world and education: How America's commitment to equity will determine our future.* Teachers College Press.

Dimich, N., Erkens, C., Miller, J., Schimmer, T., & White, K. (2022). *Concise answers to frequently asked questions about assessment & grading.* Solution Tree.

Domina, T., Hanselman, P., Hwang, N., & McEachin, A. (2016, August). Tracking and tracking up: Mathematics in California middle schools, 2003–2013. *American Educational Research Journal, 53*(4), 1229–1266.

Doubet, K. (2022). *The flexibly grouped classroom: How to organize learning for equity and growth.* ASCD.

Draeger, C., & Wilson, D. (2016, March 8). How to give students more control over their learning. *Education Week.* https://www.edweek.org/teaching-learning/opinion-how-to-give-students-more-control-over-their-learning/2016/03

DuFour, R., & Eaker, R. (1998). *Professional learning communities at work: Best practices for enhancing student achievement.* Solution Tree.

Dweck, C. (2000). *Self theories: Their role in motivation, personality, and development.* Psychology Press.

Dweck, C. (2006). *Mindset: The new psychology of success.* Random House.

Dweck, C. (2017). *Mindset: Changing the way you think to fulfill your potential.* Random House.

Earl, L. (2013). *Assessment as learning: Using classroom assessment to maximize student learning* (2nd ed.). Corwin.

Educational Research Service. (1993). *Academic challenge for the children of poverty.* Author.

Erickson, H., Lanning, L., & French, R. (2017). *Concept-based curriculum & instruction for the thinking classroom* (2nd ed.). Corwin.

Ervin, S. (2022, March 8). 5 ways to de-escalate challenging student behavior. *ASCD Blog.* https://www.ascd.org/blogs/5-ways-to-de-escalate-challenging-student-behavior

Fullan, M. (2001a). *Leading in a culture of change.* Jossey-Bass.

Fullan, M. (2001b). *The new meaning of educational change* (3rd ed.). Teachers College Press.

Fullan, M. (2008). *Six secrets of change: What the best leaders do to help their organizations survive and thrive.* Jossey-Bass.

Fullan, M., Quinn, J., & McEachan, J. (2018). *Deep learning: Engage the world, change the world.* Corwin.

Gardner, J. (1961). *Excellence: Can we be equal and excellent too?* Harper & Row.

Gobir, N. (2021, May 25). How unconditional positive regard can help students feel cared for. *MindShift.* https://www.kqed.org/mindshift/57646/how-unconditional-positive-regard-can-help-students-feel-cared-for

Good, C., Aronson, J., & Inzlicht, M. (2003). Improving adolescents' standardized test performance: An intervention to reduce the effects of stereotype threat. *Applied Developmental Psychology, 24*, 645–662.

Gorsky, P. (2018). *Reaching and teaching students in poverty: Strategies for erasing the opportunity gap.* Teachers College Press.

Greene, R. (2014). *Lost at school: Why our kids with behavioral challenges are falling through the cracks and how we can help them.* Scribner.

Greene, R. (2021a). *Lost & found: Unlocking collaboration and compassion to help our most vulnerable, misunderstood students (and all the rest)* (2nd ed.). Jossey-Bass.

Greene, R. (2021b). *The explosive child* (6th ed.). Harper.

Guskey, T. (1994, October). Making the grade: What benefits students? *Educational Leadership, 52*(2), 14–20.

Guskey, T. (2020, September). Breaking up the grade. *Educational Leadership, 78*(1), 40–46.

Guskey, T. (2019, October 28). Grades versus comments: Research on student feedback. *Kappan.* https://kappanonline.org/grades-versus-comments-researchstudent-feedback-guskey/

Guskey, T., & Brookhart, S. (2019). *What we know about grading: What works, what doesn't, and what's next?* ASCD.

Haberman, M. (1991). The pedagogy of poverty versus good teaching. *Phi Delta Kappan, 73*(4), 290–294.

Hattie, J. (2009). *Visible learning: A synthesis of 800+ meta-analyses on achievement.* Routledge.

Hattie, J. (2012). *Visible learning for teachers: Maximizing impact on learning.* Routledge.

Hattie, J. (2017). *Backup of Hattie's ranking list of 256 influences and effect sizes related to student achievement.* https://visible-learning.org/backup-hattie-ranking-256-effects-2017

Hodges, H. (2001). Overcoming a pedagogy of poverty. In R. W. Cole (Ed.), *More strategies for educating everybody's children* (pp. 1–9). ASCD.

Hopfenberg, W., & Levin, H. (2008). *The accelerated schools resource guide.* Jossey-Bass.

Jepsen, C. (2015). Class size: Does it matter for student achievement? *World of Labor.* https://wol.iza.org/articles/class-size-does-it-matter-for-student-achievement/long

Kafele, B. (2021). *The equity and social justice education 50: Critical questions for improving opportunities and outcomes for Black students.* ASCD.

Katz, I., & Assor, A. (2007). When choice motivates and when it does not. *Educational Psychology Review, 19*(4), 429–444.

Kopp, W. (2001). *One day, all children . . . The unlikely triumph of Teach for America and what I learned along the way.* Perseus Books.

LePage, P., Darling-Hammond, L., & Akar, H. (2005). Classroom management. In L. Darling-Hammond & J. Bransford (Eds.), *Preparing teachers for a changing world: What teachers should learn and be able to do* (pp. 327–357). Jossey-Bass.

Lieberman, M. (2020, May 5). Stop giving inexperienced teachers all the lower-level math classes, reformers argue. *Education Week.* https://www.edweek.org/teaching-learning/stop-giving-inexperienced-teachers-all-the-lower-level-math-classes-reformers-argue/2020/05

Lynch, M. (2015, October 9). The first year teaching: Classroom rules and routines. *The Edvocate.* https://www.theedadvocate.org/the-first-year-teaching-classroom-rules-and-routines/

Marzano, R. J. (2009, September). Setting the record straight on "high-yield" strategies. *Kappan, 91*(1), 30–37.

Marzano, R. J., Marzano, J. S., & Pickering, D. J. (2003). *Classroom management that works: Research-based strategies for every teacher.* ASCD.

Maslow, A. H. (1943). A theory of human motivation. *Psychological Review, 50*(4), 370–396.

McCombs, B., & Whisler, J. S. (1997). *The lesson-centered classroom and school: Strategies for increasing student motivation and achievement.* Jossey-Bass.

McTighe, J., Doubet, K., & Carbaugh, E. (2020). *Designing authentic performance tasks and projects: Tools for meaningful learning and assessment.* ASCD.

National Association for the Education of Young Children. (2019). Advocating equity in early childhood education: *Position statement.* https://www.naeyc.org/resources/position-statements/equity

National Association for the Education of Young Children. (2020). Developmentally appropriate practice. *Position statement.* https://www.naeyc.org/resources/position-statements/dap/contents

National Association of Secondary School Principals. (2018). *Building ranks: A comprehensive framework for effective school leaders.* Author.

National Board for Professional Teaching Standards. (2010). *Mathematics standards* (3rd ed.). Author. https://www.nbpts.org/wp-content/uploads/2021/09/EAYA-MATH.pdf

National Board for Professional Teaching Standards. (2014). *English language arts standards* (3rd ed.). Author. https://www.nbpts.org/wp-content/uploads/2021/09/EAYA-ELA.pdf

National Research Council. (2000). *How people learn: Brain, mind, experience, and school.* National Academies Press.

Ng, B. (2018, January). The neuroscience of growth mindset and intrinsic motivation. *Brain Sciences, 8*(2), 20. https://www.ncbi.nlm.nih.gov/pmc/articles/PMC5836039/

O'Connor, K. (2017). *How to grade for learning: Linking grades to standards* (4th ed.). Corwin.

O'Connor, K. (2022). *A repair kit for grading: 15 fixes for broken grades* (3rd ed.). FIRST Educational Resources.

O'Keefe, P., Dweck, C., & Walton, G. (2018, September 10). Having a growth mindset makes it easier to develop new interests. *Harvard Business Review.* https://hbr.org/2018/09/having-a-growth-mindset-makes-it-easier-to-develop-new-interests

Olson, K. (2009). *Wounded by school: Recapturing the joy in learning and standing up to old school culture.* Teachers College Press.

Paley, V. G. (1993). *You can't say you can't play.* Harvard University Press.

Parker, F., Novak, J., & Bartell, T. (2017). To engage students, give them meaningful choices in the classroom. *Phi Delta Kappan 99*(2), 37–41.

Paul, A. (2013, November 4). How the power of interest drives learning. *MindShift.* https://www.kqed.org/mindshift/32503/how-the-power-of-interest-drives-learning

Rosen, J. (2016, March 30). Teacher expectations reflect racial biases, Johns Hopkins study suggests. *The Hub.* https://hub.jhu.edu/2016/03/30/racial-bias-teacher-expectations-black-white/

Rothstein-Fisch, C., & Trumbull, E. (2008). *Managing diverse classrooms: How to build on students' cultural strengths.* ASCD.

Schlechty, P. (1997). *Inventing better schools: An action plan for educational reform.* Jossey-Bass.

Sizer, T. (1985). *Horace's compromise: The dilemma of the American high school.* Houghton-Mifflin.

Smith, D., Fisher, D., & Frey, N. (2015). *Better than carrots or sticks: Restorative discipline practices for positive classroom management.* ASCD.

Sousa, D., & Tomlinson, C. (2018). *Differentiation and the brain: How neuroscience supports the learner-friendly classroom* (2nd ed). Solution Tree.

Sparks, S. (2021, April 9). "Growth mindset" linked to higher test scores, student well-being in global study. *Education Week.* https://www.edweek.org/leadership/growth-mindset-linked-to-higher-test-scores-student-well-being-in-global-study/2021/04

Spiegel, A. (2012, September 17). Teachers' expectations can influence how students perform. https://www.npr.org/sections/health-shots/2012/09/18/161159263/teachers-expectations-can-influence-how-students-perform

Stronge, J. (2018). *Qualities of effective teachers* (3rd ed.). ASCD.

Tomlinson, C. (2014). *The differentiated classroom: Responding to the needs of all learners* (2nd ed). ASCD.

Tomlinson, C. (2017). *How to differentiate instruction in academically diverse classrooms* (3rd ed.). ASCD.

Tomlinson, C. (2021). *So each may soar: The principles and practices of learner-centered classrooms.* ASCD.

Tomlinson, C. (2022). *Everybody's classroom: Differentiating for the shared and unique needs of diverse students.* Teachers College Press.

Tomlinson, C., & Doubet, K. (2005, April). Reach them to teach them. *Educational Leadership, 62*(7), 9–15.

Tomlinson, C., & McTighe, J. (2006). *Integrating differentiated instruction & understanding by design: Connecting content and kids.* ASCD.

Tomlinson, C., & Moon, T. (2013). *Assessment and student success in a differentiated classroom.* ASCD.

Tomlinson, C., & Murphy, M. (2015). *Leading for differentiation: Growing teachers who grow kids.* ASCD.

Tomlinson, C. A., Kaplan, S. N., Renzulli, J. S., Purcell, J. H, Leppien, J. H., Burns, D. E., Strickland, C. A., & Imbeau, M. B. (2009). *The parallel curriculum: A design to develop learner potential and challenge advanced learners.* Corwin.

Toth, M. D., & Sousa, D. (2019). *The power of student teams: Achieving social, emotional, and cognitive learning in every classroom through academic teaming.* Learning Sciences International.

Truong, D. (2022, May 17). Detracking in K–12 classes. *U.S. News & World Report.* https://www.usnews.com/education/k12/articles/detracking-in-k-12-classrooms

Villa, R., & Thousand, J. (2005). *Creating an inclusive school* (2nd ed.). ASCD.

Vygotsky, L. S. (1978). *Mind in society.* Harvard University Press.

Vygotsky, L. S. (1986). *Thought and language.* MIT Press.

Ware, F. (2006). Warm demander pedagogy: Culturally responsive teaching that supports a culture of achievement for African American students. *Urban Education, 41*(4), 427–456.

Wiggins, G. (1992). Foreword. In R. Villa, J. Thousand, W. Stainback, & S. Stainback (Eds.), *Restructuring for caring and effective education: An administrative guide to creating heterogeneous schools* (pp. xv–xvi). Paul H. Brookes.

Wiggins, G. (1993). *Assessing student performance.* Jossey-Bass.

Wiggins, G., & McTighe, J. (2005). *Understanding by design* (2nd ed.). ASCD.

Wiliam, D. (2011). *Embedded formative assessment.* Solution Tree.

Zhao, Y. (2009). *Catching up or leading the way: American education in the age of globalization.* ASCD

Zhao, Y. (2022). *Learners without borders: New learning pathways for all students.* Corwin.

Index

The letter *f* following a page locator denotes a figure.

About the Authors

Carol Ann Tomlinson is William Clay Parrish Jr. Professor Emeritus at the University of Virginia's School of Education and Human Development, where she served as Chair of Educational Leadership, Foundations, and Policy and Co-Director of the University's Institutes on Academic Diversity. Prior to joining the faculty at UVa, she was a teacher in public schools for 21 years, during which she taught students in high school, preschool, and middle school and also administered programs for struggling and advanced learners. She was Virginia's Teacher of the Year in 1974.

Tomlinson is author of over 300 books, book chapters, articles, and other educational materials including *How to Differentiate Instruction in Academically Diverse Classrooms, The Differentiated Classroom: Responding to the Needs of All Learners, Differentiation and the Brain: How Neuroscience Supports the Learner-Friendly Classroom* (with David Sousa), *So Each May Soar: The Principles and Practices of Learner-Centered Classrooms*, and *Everybody's Classroom: Differentiating for the Shared and Unique Needs of Diverse Learners.* Her books on differentiation are available in 14 languages.

Tomlinson was named Outstanding Professor at UVa's School of Education and Human Development in 2004 and received an All-University Teaching Award in 2008. In 2022, she was ranked #12 in the *Education Week* Edu-Scholar Public Presence Rankings of the 200 "university-based academics who are contributing most substantially to public debates about schools and schooling," and as the #4 voice in Curriculum & Instruction. She works throughout the United States and internationally with educators who seek to create classrooms that are effective in reaching diverse student populations. She can be reached by email at cat3y@virginia.edu.

Marcia B. Imbeau is a professor and childhood/ elementary education program coordinator in the Department of Curriculum and Instruction at the University of Arkansas, working in its teacher preparation program. She has 40 years of experience as a classroom teacher in public schools, a coordinator of university-based summer/Saturday enrichment programs, an adjunct professor, and a presenter to teachers, instructional leaders, and administrators throughout the United States and internationally.

For the past 25 years, Imbeau has worked as a university liaison in local public schools to assist interns and their mentor teachers, a role that allows her to collaborate with public school faculty (many of them former students) to prepare new generations of K–6 educators and K–12 teachers who work with advanced learners.

Imbeau coauthored *A Differentiated Approach to the Common Core* and *Managing a Differentiated Classroom (Grades K–8)*. She worked with colleagues at the University of Arkansas on *Differentiating Instruction in the Inclusive Classroom: Strategies for Success*. These books remind readers of the principles important for differentiation and provide practical ideas teachers can use in their classrooms. Imbeau is also a coauthor of *The Parallel Curriculum* and the editor of *Parallel Curriculum Units for Grades K–5*. She can be reached by email at mimbeau@uark.edu.